BEHAVIOR *Self*
THE HARD CASE FOR SOFT SKILLS

*How to cultivate a culture of civility through good behaviors
to improve the workplace and overall well- being*

AMBER ROSE COX

Emotional Intelligence Specialist/ Coach/Global Trainer, Presenter

Copyright 2021 by Amber Rose Cox

Printed in the United States of America

First Printing 2021

ISBN: 9798701256864

Contact Amber Rose Cox at:

amber@workculturesolutions.com
www.workculturesolutions.com

AMBER ROSE COX

Amber is a client directed change expert whose work

has been recognized nationally. Her work encompasses

incorporating cohesive relationships and behavioral change according to goals, desires, and general well-being for individuals, teams, and companies. As a facilitator of change, she uses integrative modalities and processes such as emotional intelligence (EI) training, neuro-linguistic programming (NLP), and hypnosis.

Amber is a global presenter and trainer on Emotional Intelligence. She leads workshops and delivers training on Communication Excellence and How to Be An Effective Leader. In addition, she is skilled at delivering presentations and demons-trations on the Power of Suggestion with regard to behavioral change in utilizing mindfulness, resilience, and stress reduction techniques.

Amber is a Board Certified Hypnotist and has done extensive and advanced training with leaders in the profession.

Amber has over a twenty-five-year background in corporate sales and a private hypnosis practice for the past thirteen years. She is a Maine native where she resides with her family, and two pugs.

Dedication

This book is dedicated to my amazing and supportive family who helped teach me and push me to learn about the value of positive communication and the influence it has on every aspect of our lives. Also this is for all those who are passionate about improving the human connection and making the world a happier place.

Acknowledgements

I want to thank my colleague, mentor and friend Beryl Comar for her incredible knowledge and teachings on Emotional Intelligence Development.

I also want to thank Dr. Richard Nongard for his support and mentorship so that this book exists.

And to my family, for your constant belief in me through my many endeavors and adventures, you are everything to me.

Table of Contents

Preface

As long as I can remember I have been interested in how people communicate and interact within their communication. It is the foundation of how we relate to each other and how we relate to our environment. Throughout my life and career, I have had the opportunity to observe a variety of personal and professional relationships and those interactions. I became very interested in the tremendous effect communication has on our emotional and physical health.

This interest inspired me to explore and learn as much as I could about the dynamics of verbal and nonverbal communication and how I could take that learning to help people improve their lives and their relationships.

These learnings helped me tremendously in my life by pushing my introspect and self-awareness. As I applied the simple strategies that I write about in this book to the way I interacted with family and my colleagues I found my potential for success expanded. I also increased the quality of relationships in my life and relationship with myself in a positive and more meaningful way.

It is true that many things that happen externally are out of our control. One of the most powerful things that we can control is how we think and respond to any given situation. This is the key to a happier and healthier life and also a contribution to a kinder and more compassionate world.

I sincerely hope you enjoy this book and take something from it, if only one thing and that it makes a positive difference in your life.

Introduction

What is the emotional health of your company?

This could be one of the most critical questions any organization leader or manager could ask. As you reflect on that question and read this book, think about the company you work for or perhaps the ones you have worked for in the past. If you do not know the level of your company's emotional health, survey your teams, and you will be sure to find out. It could very well be the most valuable information you collect to improve your company's livelihood, hands down.

In this book, you will find the research, logic, statistics, and solutions to help you and your company join the movement of other successful organizations that make embracing and improving the workplace a top priority.

Incorporating certain behaviors in the workplace that

are standardized should be non-negotiable, given that the emotional health of any company is significantly impacted by behavior. When behavior standards are embedded in a company's culture, they substantially impact the prosperity of the company and the emotional health of the employees. If you don't think your employees' emotional health affects the bottom line, this book will be a game-changer for you.

In my career spanning more than twenty-five years, I have thousands of hours directly observing how people interact with one another in a variety of professional settings. It's fascinating that communication seems such a simple concept but becomes the most significant barrier in relationships. Communication is everything; think about it—communication is where every relationship begins.

How we communicate to ourselves or how we are communicating with another individual, group, or team directly influences how well we thrive in life. Communication can either make or break a relationship; it also affects how we feel about ourselves in a very significant way. Our thoughts affect our emotional and physical health. How we think affects how we respond to any situation in life. They are extremely powerful and shape the experiences that we have every moment of every day.

It has been proven through research that our thoughts or self-talk can impact our physical health. The books *Biology of Belief* by Dr. Bruce Lipton, *The Body Keeps Score* by Bessel van der Kolk, and *You Are Not Your Brain*, by Jeffrey M. Schwartz MD and Rebecca Gladding MD, are fascinating reads on the subject in which they explore this concept. These are some of many books I have read and studied on the impact that our thoughts and self talk have on our bodies health. Also, I have spent years observing people and their interactions with one another in the corporate and medical field and my own private practice. The most obvious and glaring problem many businesses constantly struggle with is communication breakdowns and barriers. This commonly results in frustration, resentment, misunderstanding, turnover, and more. Understanding and learning how to develop certain skills, which are often referred to as "soft skills," have been proven to impact a greater level of success in desired outcomes. Some of the many outcomes improved include productivity, happier and more engaged employees and customers, employee and customer retention, and several other benefits that will be examined throughout this book.

For years I have been fostering solutions to address the area of how people behave and the competency of their behavior or soft skills. These solutions embody behaviors that encompass respect, listening, empathy, and compassion. Developing soft skills is also referred to as developing a person's "Emotional Intelligence," which will be covered more in the following chapters. Incivility or toxic work cultures are often overlooked by leadership and are staggeringly costly to any company. This type of environment takes a toll on the company's emotional health, which depends on people's emotional health. I have witnessed hundreds of people suffer and be miserable due to a lack of standards of behavior in the workplace culture throughout my career.

The most valuable asset of any business is the people. One would naturally think that this area would be a primary focus for development and standards. Yet, it is more often than not overlooked. Unfortunately, I have observed more people that are very unhappy with their work environment, boss, or team than are happy. Since our environment directly impacts a person's health and well-being, there is a huge opportunity to develop this area of focus. In this book, you will read easy and proven step-by-step behaviors that you can implement to improve your work's culture and emotional health.

These behaviors can be utilized within any company, organization, or business. They can also be used in daily life to improve relationships and communication. If you are in any business that involves sustaining relationships and enhancing communication, you will benefit from these behaviors. Even implementing one or two of the evidence-based and best practices will make an improvement. Companies that have embraced developing soft skills soon realize the potential of investing in this area. I appreciate this quote from John Dewey, who was regarded as one of the greatest American philosophers and one of the most prominent American scholars in the first half of the twentieth century: "The deepest urge in human nature is the desire to be important."

My hope for you in reading this book is that it inspires you to implement some of these behaviors or soft skills, and you enjoy it. At the core of every human being is a natural need and desire to connect, feel heard, and valued. That is what this book is all about. It is the common threads that unite us as human beings, naturally wanting and needing authentic human connection and understanding.

Chapter 1

Slowing Down To Go Faster

It is all too common that when we have heavy workloads, we naturally feel the need to rush through to get everything done. When we are in a position of serving other people in some capacity, rushing can incur more cost as attention to detail may get lost. We may miss some essential information that could result in more time spent fixing something or a situation, or worst-case scenario, compromise the physical or emotional well being of the person to whom we are providing a service.

Mary and Tom's story demonstrates a valuable lesson for everyone. Mary grabbed Tom's hand and squeezed tightly as Tom drove them frantically to the hospital's emergency department. Mary was feeling her heart race in her chest, and her head was spinning. Something was off with her, and she intuitively felt it since her recent gallbladder surgery. Thoughts were flying through Mary's head, and she was reflecting on her care during her recent overnight stay at the hospital. She had been a bit confused about the medication prescribed and the aftercare. Mary had been admitted and rushed to the operating room so fast everything was a blur. She didn't have time to process the post-surgery instructions completely but was assured she was well enough to be discharged and go home. Thoughts raced through Mary's mind; she kept wondering if she had taken the medication incorrectly or perhaps forgot some part of her aftercare instructions. As Tom pulled up to the hospital's emergency department doors, Mary felt weaker; her head was spinning, and her legs felt numb. Tom rushed around to help her out of the car, and Mary collapsed at the door.

The medical staff ran out and quickly put Mary on a stretcher, rushing her in as Tom quickly followed. Tom was confused about what was happening; a week ago, Mary was fine. Then she had an emergency gallbladder operation and since felt off.

After Mary's surgery, the hospital staff discharged her with some instructions for an antibiotic and some physical limitations. Tom and Mary were reassured that Mary would heal fine and be back to normal within a few weeks.

Now, Tom could not imagine what could have gone wrong; Mary had been feeling off for the past couple of days, not feeling well, and had developed chills and a low fever. Her symptoms worsened, and her fever spiked, and the hospital medical staff advised her to go to the local emergency department. As Tom waited for what seemed like hours, a doctor finally returned and told him Mary would be okay, but unfortunately, she had an allergic reaction to the medication prescribed.

Tom was horrified; it should have been in all of Mary's records that she had specific allergies to a few antibiotics. How could this have happened? How could they have missed this? So many questions were going through Tom's head, and at the same time, he was grateful that Mary would recover.

This scenario is not uncommon in the medical field. In the story above, the medication prescribed caused an allergic reaction, and, for some reason, the allergy to the medication had been missed by the medical staff. Doctors, nurses, and clinicians are pushed to be more productive and see more patients. The way medicine is delivered has changed significantly, and the demands of the technological world weigh heavily with time constraints. Time spent with patients has decreased; patients are discharged more quickly, including after significant surgeries. The whole system has become very complicated. This all takes away from time actually spent with a patient and hits home as patient safety and outcome are directly impacted. In the medical field, one of the most important factors, along with the delivery of traditional medicine, is the delivery of emotional care, which is a major influence and component on how the relationship with the patient develops or deteriorates.

Things like being present, listening, making eye contact, reassuring the patient, checking for a clear understanding of the plan of care are behaviors, when not paid attention to because of time constraints and rushing, not only affect the bottom line but, more importantly, can affect a patient's safety. Errors can occur, as well as a rise in readmittance rates, and some mistakes result in costly litigation. Research shows that patients are way less likely to pursue a lawsuit in the medical field if they like their patient care experience, even if something goes wrong. If a patient has a good relationship with their medical provider and team, it creates relatability and loyalty. Taking a few extra minutes for the medical staff to slow down could have prevented harm to Mary in the scenario above and avoided a potential lawsuit. Take a look at these statistics around litigation.

In the time it takes you to read this sentence, roughly US$7,000 was spent on medical malpractice in the United States alone. Let that settle in for a moment. That number is based on a Health Affairs study that estimated annual medical malpractice related costs to reach approximately US$55.6 billion, or 2.4% of total healthcare spending. That startling number does not include all defensive medicine costs like prescribing unwarranted tests and treatments to avoid lawsuits. Money spent exclusively on medical malpractice lawsuit payouts topped a staggering US$3 billion in 2012, according to *Forbes*.

Unfortunately, medicine has become more of a business of profitability, and patients' care has become secondary in many cases. This is a result of the changing nature and demands on healthcare and healthcare providers. If standards of behaviors were prioritized and embedded into the medical world's culture and training, millions of dollars would be saved, and most notably, lives. It is a tough place for a physician to be in; most physicians get into medicine because it is a calling and their passion to help people. It brings them joy, so the arduous medical school journey and the long hours that go with that are part of the experience.

However, what has happened is that the medical profession has become saddled with so many other tasks that take time away from facing patients. Amongst tasks taking time away from direct patient care are charting, documenting, inputting data, dealing with complex insurances, learning the computer software systems, and productivity goals, to name a few. All of these extra technical mechanics or hard skills have created a strain on our medical providers. Our high-speed computerized world tasks have added additional responsibilities that are not as focused on the patient.

This results in a decline in the joy and fulfillment of why doctors and clinicians chose this field. Physician burnout is more prevalent than ever now.

Physician burnout predicts physician turnover, which has a high cost and impact on the community. At Stanford Medicine, replacing a physician who leaves because of burnout can cost at least US$250,000. This does not take into account the economic impacts on the community. Implementing behaviors into an organization that takes into consideration the emotional well being and health of the physicians is a pressing situation. Addressing the organizational factors that contribute to burnout is more than just a question of the bottom line; it is necessary to the providers' and clinicians' health and well-being. Attending to the well-being of physicians and clinicians supports and affects better patient relationships and safer outcomes. If the medical staff is experiencing burnout, it is more challenging to connect with patients, give proper attention, and spend quality time with them.

Attention to detail declines due to increased stress and pressure with the increasing demands in this profession.

The medical field is not the only business suffering from a lack of standards of behaviors. This affects the corporate world in a big way; any business that involves people and relationships is greatly affected by behavior. Research also shows that people who are happy and enjoying their jobs are less likely to leave and are much more productive. Happy and engaged employees and a positive work environment foster creativity, performance, and team spirit. This also transfers to how well employees treat their customers.

Solutions to these challenges lie in attention, education, and training focused on specific non-negotiable behavior standards. Also important is having everyone involved be accountable to those standards that exhibit an inclusive culture so that everyone's input is considered important. Developing a systematic approach is a critical piece of improving the work culture and having better employee and client relationships. In doing this, the emotional health and stability of the workplace are addressed, and opportunities open to improving the well- being of the entire company.

Below are some statistics on incivility (or a lack of

good behaviors) in the workplace. This information results from a poll of 800 managers and employees in 17 industries on workplace relationships. These are compelling statistics from a book on emotional intelligence by an internationally known psychologist and recognized leader in the field, Daniel Goleman.

Following are the results of employees' behaviors that experienced forms of incivility.

- 48% intentionally decreased their work effort.

- 47% intentionally decreased the time spent at work.

- 38% intentionally decreased the quality of their work.

- 80% lost work time worrying about incidents or situations.

- 63% lost work time avoiding the situation.

- 66% said that their performance declined.

- 78% said that their commitment to the organization declined.

- 12% said that they left their job because of incivility.

Unfortunately, incivility in the workplace culture is way more common than you might think. According to poll results in Daniel Goleman's book *Emotional Intelligence,* incivility in the workplace is on the rise and has increased over the past several years. In polling thousands of workers, it was reported that a whopping 98% experienced some form of incivility.

I have witnessed incivility and toxic work environments or culture countless times throughout my career. I have seen numerous people in my private practice suffering from emotional distress due to this. The emotional distress results in physical challenges such as insomnia, headaches, high blood pressure, and muscle tension. It also affects the ability to interact with other people in a grounded manner.

Relationships become strained and reactive, causing all kinds of problems that extend into a person's private life. It is sad for me to say this, but I have found that it is much more common that people are unhappy or dissatisfied with their work environment.

Some of my career has been in the medical profession as a coach. Nurses bullying each other was a huge issue and, unfortunately, still is. There is a saying in the field that "Nurses eat their young." I know that sounds terrible, but it is a very well known expression. Even in nursing school, that expression is discussed with the students. Recently one of my daughter's best friends who graduated from nursing school explored this expression and confirmed that nursing students were cautioned about bullying.

Jill, a veteran nurse, had a heartbreaking story. She had suffered for years with bullying in her assigned nursing department, and as she challenged behaviors, the bullying got worse. She moved around within the organization to different specialties and floors and found bullying was still prevalent. Ultimately, Jill decided to leave her career as the emotional distress was causing health problems. This was a career in which she had invested her heart and soul. Years of training and a passion for helping others was what she felt her calling always was. Deciding to become a nurse for Jill was easy, but being a nurse was very different. For Jill, it was not about the physical demands or the emotional challenges of caring for sick patients; it was the people in her work environment. The colleagues that she thought would support and be a source of comfort and understanding turned out to be the most challenging aspect of the job. Every day was a struggle for Jill to maintain her sense of self, remembering why she made the decision to work in the medical field. Jill experienced other nurses to be highly competitive, judgmental, insulting, and critical. I am in no way generalizing nurses. There are many nurses that are wonderful. I have witnessed and experienced both types of nurses in my professional and personal life. However, nurse bullying is a huge problem and acknowledged within the nursing field, with much research and information corroborating its presence. Jill ultimately pursued a lawsuit, which unfortunately led to additional emotional distress. She felt litigation was her best recourse and a chance to bring her voice to what she had experienced and witnessed.

Had the concept of non-negotiable behaviors been applied, it would have prevented a myriad of behavioral issues that affected not only Jill's ability but the ability of other colleagues to do their jobs effectively. Jill went on to become an advocate for behavior standards in the nursing profession.

Although I reference this story that is specific to the medical profession, it is something that goes on in many work environments. Every environment that is in the business of people and relationships is affected by behavior. Incivility can take many forms. Here are some examples:

Behaviors of Incivility in the Workplace

Insults

Belittling

Blaming

Door slamming

Side conversations

Exclusion

Disregard for a person's time

Overly controlling management

Subtler Forms of Incivility

Taking credit for someone else's work

Emailing or texting in a meeting or presentation

Teasing in a hurtful way

All of these behaviors take a considerable toll on the emotional health of employees. In turn, that toll is reflected in the company's performance and the overall company's emotional health and stability.

Impact of Incivility with an Organization's Employees

Lower work effort and productivity

Less attention to detail, resulting in increased errors

Turnover resulting in increased hiring and training costs

Retaliation or litigation

Resentment and team deterioration

Low morale

Also impacted are the effects on customer relationship, and customer satisfaction as employees' frustrations are projected when they are subjected to this type of behavior.

The question remains, where does one start in turning this around? What are the essential actions your organization needs to do to begin the process of shifting the behaviors?

It starts with the people and everybody embracing and embedding behaviors that are made a priority and held as important as the hard skills or technical skills.

Taking the emotional culture seriously and understanding that its impacts are deep and wide in an organization is first and foremost. Implementing education and training at every level that is focused on behavior standards or soft skills will support that these behaviors are embedded in the culture and modeled as the overall goal of increasing employee, client, customer, and patient engagement and experience.

As you continue reading the next pages, you will learn more about the importance of behavior standards and how to apply soft skills in any industry across the board with every level of employee and customer. You will be astounded at the positive impact it will have on your team and company's health and wealth. I will also provide solutions in the coming chapters that you can easily apply.

Chapter 2

Defining Work Culture and Emotional Intelligence

Good behavior standards in the workplace are not to be ignored or considered a luxury any longer. How people behave in the workplace sets the tone of the culture, and how people behave and treat each other directly impacts any company's success.

Attitudes are contagious, and people tend to follow or mirror their managers' and leaders' behaviors for guidance for acceptable behavior. Emotional intelligence development or soft skill development is all about how people behave, how they socially and emotionally relate to other people. More and more research and evidence are surfacing in supporting how vital this area of focus and development is. If your company's business involves relationships, it is wise to incorporate and invest in training. This could save thousands of dollars by directly impacting a company's ability to perform, grow, and ultimately be more profitable.

For starters, let's define what work culture is: It is a concept which deals in the study of beliefs, thought processes, and attitudes of the leaders and employees. A good work culture is one that inspires employees to always respect, support, help, and encourage one another. I am sure you have heard of "the work-family." Like a supportive family, everyone has each other's backs in a supportive work-family culture. This culture can only be successful when the company leaders model these values. Leaders set the corporate behavioral tone and establish which behaviors are acceptable and not acceptable. One of the reasons that the responsibility is primarily on leadership is because their behavior and attitudes get magnified and mirrored throughout the organization. People talk and are quick to share if they are unhappy with their environment or leaders. The price of incivility is not only costly in productivity but hurts morale and employee engagement. Emotional intelligence development or soft skills development is the foundation of good communication, understanding, transparency, and cohesiveness of relationships in any environment. Research shows that it is a skill that can propel the success of any organization. Emotional intelligence is all about creating awareness in self to regulate behavior with individuals or groups. It is not just another handy set of feel-good skills; it is a game-changer that more successful companies embrace and incorporate. According to an article in *Psychology Today*, the definition of emotional intelligence is: "Emotional intelligence refers to the ability to identify and manage one's own emotions, as well as the emotions of others."

Emotional intelligence (EI) for any person is as or more important in life, and some would argue more important than a person's intelligence quotient (IQ). The intelligence quotient does not change much through a person's life, but EI can be learned and developed. Have you ever met a person that you just instantly felt a connection with, that you knew they were really listening to you and seemed to *get you*?

Immediately, you felt comfortable with them and thought that talking with them was very easy. If you, like many people, have had this experience, you have likely also experienced the opposite. Think of another time when you met someone, and the encounter felt awkward, and the conversation was a struggle. The difference between the two often comes down to a person's EI competency. The foundation of emotional intelligence can be broken down into four quadrants. These are taken from Daniel Goleman's book, *Emotional Intelligence*.

Emotional Intelligence 4 Quadrants

Self Awareness

The ability to become aware of and know your emotions and triggers.

Self Regulation

The ability to be in control of your emotions for a positive outcome.

Social Awareness

The ability to be aware of the mood of an individual or team.

<u>Relationship Management</u>

The ability to navigate relationships by employing the other quadrants.

Think of emotions as the driver of behavior. People respond to either internal or external dialogue, situations, or events. Learning how to become aware of and regulate those emotions effectively is the key to having more internal and external control and a sense of peace. Consider that emotions are data points and answer the questions below.

Check which of these emotions resulted in any of these:

Check which of these emotions you have felt recently	Check which experiences have resulted
☐ Frustration	☐ Poor communication
☐ Irritability	☐ Wasted time
☐ Anxiety	☐ Stress
☐ Annoyance	☐ Poor teamwork
☐ Anger	☐ Headaches
☐ Loneliness	☐ Sleepless nights
☐ Tiredness	☐ Muscle tension
☐ Sadness	☐ Stomachaches

This exercise demonstrates the direct impact that emotions have on our physical health. When we experience a continual upset in our emotional state, it can result in increased stress. When people are chronically stressed, it affects their ability to think clearly, act reasonably, and creates physical challenges. I will explain more about stress and the importance of managing it in Chapter 11.

Many great leaders have average or above IQ, but a significant contributor to their success with people is because they are high on the EQ skillset. Leaders that embrace these behaviors are very good at self-awareness and regulating how they respond. They are also very good at managing their emotions with other people.

Managing and regulating emotions is key to positively influencing and motivating people.

Changing communication in any relationship is to become aware of yourself, your feelings, emotions, and triggers. Once you are aware of those, you can learn to regulate your emotions. This is incredibly important for leaders as everyone takes on the leaders' emotional atmosphere, which, in turn, makes up the organization's culture. Leading by example or role modeling excellent behavior sets the tone for the entire company. Any great leader has understood the significance of this. Some of the most outstanding leaders are the ones that understand the importance of good behavior and incorporating emotional intelligence skills to inspire and motivate their employees.

Here are some examples of leaders that model good behavior and have what is considered to be a high level of emotional intelligence.

John Donahoe (eBay): Donahoe's leadership style, according to research has been influenced by the best-selling author of six books on leadership excellence, Jim Collins. Donahoe also incorporated strategies from well known author Bill George and his book *True North: Discover Your Authentic Leadership*. Donahoe is said to demonstrate a high level of self-awareness and listening ability. These skills helped in creating a loyal team as well as a healthy, evolving work culture. Both Jim Collins' and Bill George's books are about modeling good behavior and leading with purpose and how important these attributes are to make companies successful.

Warren Buffet (CEO Berkshire Hathaway): Buffett has been saying for a long time that IQ isn't the single defining factor to being successful. "More important than IQ," he says, "is rationality and emotional stability." Buffett is also quoted as saying, "You don't need to be a rocket scientist. Investing is not a game where the guy with the 160 IQ beats the guy with a 130 IQ. Rationality is essential," in the book, *Warren Buffett Speaks*. The average IQ score falls between 85 and 115. A score above 140 is considered a genius-level IQ. Buffet goes on to say you should "Give away 30 points to somebody else because you don't need a lot of brains to be in this business. What you do need is emotional stability." And he adds, "You have to be able to think independently."

Indra Nooyi (Pepsi): Nooyi is a conscious capitalist whose Performance with Purpose agenda has helped move employees from having a job to living a calling. She is acutely aware that being a woman of color means she may receive more attention and scrutiny. However, she still projects her personality without reservation— whether it's singing in the hallways or walking barefoot in the office.

She wrote the parents of twenty-nine senior Pepsi executives telling them what great kids they had raised.

Below are some examples of emotionally intelligent behaviors in the workplace that bring about positive change in culture.

1. Compassion and understanding. People have off days, or even bad days; it is part of life. Compassion goes a lot further than just telling someone to get over it or let it go, and having an understanding of other people's feelings models that we, too, are human and have days that don't necessarily go as we would wish. Of course, if having an off day or bad day were to become a persistent problem with a person, that would need to be addressed with more dedicated help or support.

2. Listening in meetings and other conversations without interrupting or getting distracted by texts or emails. This behavior models mutual respect for one another. Encouraging people to speak up empowers the team. When people feel confident that they can openly express their views and opinions without fear of judgment or criticism, it allows communication to flow. When people feel that it is okay to express differences, and it can be done respectfully, it allows people to feel like their thoughts are valuable and a valued contribution. When people feel that they cannot speak up, resistance builds, and communication breaks down.

3. Ability to flow with change. It is common for initiatives to change in the work environment. This can cause upset for people if they are confused as to the reason behind changing initiatives. Clear communication from leadership

in this area helps people to move with change instead of resisting it.

4. <u>Flexibility in the workplace</u>. This is incredibly important for some people and as the workplace has evolved, so has the way people are allowed to manage their time. Life and work balance have become more and more important to many people in the workplace now. A focus on lifestyle options for their professional career and support of options helps people manage their personal responsibilities. A great example is a person that has a long commute or a commute in a heavy traffic area. Given the option to come in earlier or later to avoid traffic delays helps alleviate a lot of stress for that person. Another example might be a single parent needing some flexibility around daycare hours. Leadership embracing flexibility rather than imposing a strict standard can greatly benefit from helping employees feel that the company can be flexible and give them a few options that improve their quality of life. One might think that the quality of work and productivity are independent, but many times when balanced, one improves the other. I am not making a generalization, but when people are given options around managing their workload and schedule, it sends a very different message.

5. <u>Freedom to be oneself</u>. This allows people to express themselves and tap into their strengths. Everyone brings something to the table, and you

can build on each individual's talents and strengths. In a later chapter, I am going to talk about the Nine Types of Intelligences and why it is important to understand this concept in the workplace.

6. <u>Socializing in the work environment</u>. Being social is a big part of being human. Human beings need to connect and share with one another; it is essential to our emotional health. Good camaraderie around the meeting table, in training, or at a lunch break helps people bond and get to know and learn other aspects of one another and widens the perspective of a person's personality.

7. <u>Investing in stress management</u>. Having a strategy for offering employees a way to proactively deal with stress and manage it is essential to success. Some ways to do this are relaxation or meditation sessions during lunch hours, encouraging employees to step away from the work environment go for a walk during breaks and lunches. You can also brighten the work environment with positive visuals or messages, acknowledge the progress, achievements, and goals of individuals and teams.

8. <u>Feedback from everyone. E</u>very position and role has a different view of how things are done because everyone is different and thinks and processes differently. Being open to receiving constructive feedback on what people like or prefer or around what is not working are valuable

conversations. This is important in fostering a positive work culture. It encourages everyone an opportunity to contribute to the team and company goals.

As you continue reading, I will describe behaviors that can, when implemented, provide solutions to improve emotional intelligence, behaviors, and workplace culture. You will also find this information valuable in your everyday life. Learning how to become self-aware and regulate emotions can make a significant difference in the quality of your professional and personal life.

Some of these behaviors are evidenced-based and incorporated as best practices in the medical field as a proven way to succeed in this area. Best-in-class hospitals such as The Beryl Institute and Cleveland Clinic are examples of making behaviors a standard, rated best-in-class because the teams walk the talk.

Chapter 3

The Peter Principle

The Peter Principle observation is that people tend to rise to "their level of incompetence" in a hierarchy. As people are promoted, they become progressively less effective because good performance in one job does not guarantee similar performance in another.

In my hundreds of hours of professional observations and personal experience as well as research on this subject, I have found it true that many people get promoted primarily on how competent they are at doing their job or their hard skill set. Often promotions involve that the person being promoted is managing other people. What is not taken into consideration is that not all people know how to manage people or themselves, and this difference can make or break any team. This is a particular skill set and one that can be learned and developed. Hence the research reflecting that the number one reason people quit or leave their jobs is because they are unhappy with their boss, according to a Gallup poll.

The business of leading and managing people is a delicate balance. How do you bring out the best in your team and their strengths? How do you motivate, inspire, and engage them? When a person is promoted, and these areas are overlooked or not tended to, it is a double whammy. Not only does the team suffer from an untrained manager, but the manager is set up for a world of frustration. I have witnessed countless times throughout my career that so many people feel like what they think or suggest regarding their workflow and work challenges goes unheard or doesn't matter. As human beings, we are naturally wired to want to connect with one another and feel heard and valued. In many work cultures, the focus is more weighted on operational aspects and not on employee experience and culture. This is where considerable opportunity exists actually to increase productivity and profitability. Also a high focus and priority is spent on customer or patient satisfaction, but in reality to effectively influence this aspect the people providing the services must be attended to.

When people feel like they are just a number or a "cog in the wheel," they are not emotionally invested in the outcomes. Sure they may do an average or good job, but usually, they just show up and do what they need to get by and clock their time. Have you ever been in a situation where you were miserable because of a leader's behavior? I sure have, and it was very unpleasant. I want to share a story with you from my early career experience.

I still remember her after years of trying to forget her. Her name was Susan, and she made a lasting impression on me. I was working in product development at the time for a well-known Maine-based company. I loved what I was learning and felt inspired by the desire to learn as much as I could with the opportunity to express my creativity. At the time, I was newly separated and a single working mother. Working at this company for about three years, I had been promoted a few times, initially having started in administration and promoted to product development. The experience I gained over the three years was pretty good, and I had made some great workplace friends. When I got a promotion to the product development department, all seemed to be going well, and I was given additional responsibilities. At the same time, the company was going through a tremendous amount of change in upper management, and new people were coming in while many were leaving. In the product development department, a new manager was hired— Susan—and life got a lot more interesting. I had always been considered a very upbeat, easygoing person, and with regard to work history, a good, hardworking employee. I had been promoted four times over the previous three years at this company; all my performance reviews were great.

Susan, the new department manager, was a single woman in her early forties with a straightforward, no-nonsense style. There were ten others in the department, all women and none with small children. When Susan came on board, I was in the learning phase of my new role and figuring things out on my own. I would sit with other teammates, and they would help me learn what I needed to know. When I got stuck, I would seek support from the right person. This was working out okay, although in hindsight, not an optimal way to train a new person. Everyone was friendly to each other and helpful. Have you ever heard of the expression "attitudes are contagious?" Not only was I feeling like I was being treated differently by my new manager, but some of the people in the department also started to take her lead. I began feeling excluded in conversations, ignored, and my work was now constantly being criticized. The new manager's idea and expectation of me were very different from prior managers. Although in itself is okay, what was not okay was how it was or was not communicated. No matter what I did, she found fault. I was trying so hard to do a good job. Soon, I became confused and very stressed with her discontent with my work. It was very apparent that she had issues with how I was performing, but I wondered why. It also became apparent to other people in the department that she had issues with my performance. Feeling paranoid, I began documenting every tiny detail about everything that I did. I had checklist upon checklist in case she would call me into her office. I was so miserable and nervous, and having a hard time functioning. This was my livelihood; this was an opportunity I desperately needed at the time. I was fearful and put up with the confusing behavior for a while.

One day, in particular, Susan wanted an impromptu meeting, calling me into her office. As I sat in the chair in front of her desk, she pulled out notes she had been keeping about my projects, many of which I had completed or was unable to complete due to things beyond my control. I, too, had notes with me and everything I would need to update her on my projects. Susan was not happy with my work or documentation. She looked at me straight in the eyes and told me I needed to decide if I wanted a *job* or a *career*. She asserted that if I wanted a job, maybe this was not the place for me, and if I wanted a career, I needed to be more available, meaning earlier in and later out. At the time, I knew that this was not appropriate behavior; she'd had an issue with me from the beginning, and I could only guess what that might be. Had there been a standard of behavior, many of the ways Susan acted towards me would not have been allowed. Susan and I were not congruent in our values. The disparate between us was that the amount of extra work hours put in meant to Susan a more committed and career-driven employee. I needed—and valued—having office hours within the eight-to-five window to accommodate my child's daycare. Everyone else in the department seemed okay with working earlier or later, having no daycare concerns. Even though the company was not requiring me to work beyond the eight-to-five window, Susan modeled that as important. Her attitude and behavior affected everyone, and because there was no standard of behavior and respect, it continued. Although Susan was competent at her job, there was no training on behavior excellence and modeling as a standard embraced by the company.

Susan was in the position because of her hard skill

set, not her soft skills, and there was no training or check and balance system.

Shortly after, I found another job and left, feeling stressed, defeated, and having failed. There didn't appear to be any recourse within the company for me because Susan was considered very competent at her job. I was troubled by this for a long time. I remember trying so hard to do my best; it was an incredibly confusing and frustrating time. Self-doubt in my abilities was center-stage, even though I had been promoted several times and had excellent performance reviews.

This story is not uncommon. As I moved on and became involved in corporate sales and coaching, I saw this scenario repeat itself and many others. I have witnessed and heard stories from hundreds of people in different capacities of their careers with similar frustrations and feelings. Not specifically with a manager (a lot are) but within all areas of a company.

Our environment is so important to our health and well-being. Understandably, companies need well-skilled people to be successful and profitable, but profitability is compromised without behavior standards. Imagine a company's potential if just as much attention was given to soft skills development as hard skills. Imagine a work culture where all people are trained in modeling behavior standards, addressing how people are treated, respected, listened to, and included? This approach might just make our world a lot kinder.

Chapter 4

The Nine Types Of Intelligences and Why They Matter

In this chapter, I discuss the importance of

understanding different intelligences and how understanding this concept can help companies and teams thrive. In 1983, Howard Gardener, an American developmental psychologist and a research professor of cognition and education at the Harvard Graduate School of Education at Harvard University, came up with the concept that people have other types of intelligences and that those should be acknowledged. For years the acknowledged types of intelligences have focused primarily on mathematical and linguistic meaning that in many learning institutions, the focus was on people's ability to become very competent with numbers and language. Subjects such as Math and English often were the high priority of focus and a person's aptitude or natural ability to be good in this area. In Gardener's concept and work, he showed that it was very limiting with regard to developing a person's strengths and potential contributions and overlooked many people's natural talent and abilities. Gardener's concept also represents the significant impact of understanding the other intelligences on a person's learning style and how they process and comprehend information. Gardener has published many books on this subject, some of which are considered to be quite controversial.

I included this chapter because I agree with Gardner's work. It resonates with me with regard to how I learn and process and several people that I have spoken with over my many years observing people in a variety of positions.

The 9 Intelligences that Gardener's concept includes are:

1. Logical-Mathematical

Intelligence (Number/Reasoning Smart) People that have a natural ability and tendency to solve problems with reasoning and numbers or patterns. Also, they are able to solve complex mathematical problems and are logical thinkers. Examples of positions that require this type of intelligence are programmers, analysts, and architects.

2. Linguistic Intelligence (Word Smart)

People that embody linguistic intelligence are naturally great at learning new languages. They enjoy reading and writing and also very competent at using language to accomplish goals. People that exhibit a high intelligence in linguistics and do well are public speakers, coaches, poets, and people that are great debaters and know how to use persuasive or influential language. They can also explain things well.

3. **Naturalist (Nature Smart)**

People that are of naturalist intelligence are focused on things of nature. They like being outside, are interested in plants and vegetables and how to grow them and be naturally good at it. They also may be interested in the weather patterns and environmental concerns and the well-being of the planet. Some well-known people that would be considered naturalist are: Jane Goodall, Steve Erwin, and Jacques Cousteau.

4. **Musical (Sound Smart)**

People that have a tenancy to think more in rhythms and melody as well as sensitive to music and can feel it. Someone that enjoys singing and songwriting, playing instruments, or composing is an example of musical intelligence. The ability to recognize musical patterns is also a quality of a person who is naturally of musical intelligence. I will use my oldest daughter as an excellent example of being musical smart. When she was around five years old she started playing piano by ear. We were amazed to see this little girl listen to a song playing and be able to play it by ear on the piano. She has the ability to hear music and understand pitch, tone, and inflection that is astounding.

5. <u>Existential Intelligence life smart (Spiritual / Psychic Existential)</u>

These people have a tendency to be very in tune with their intuition for operating through life. They are very sensitive to how they *feel* about the meaning of life and a connection to things greater. Pondering the meaning of existence and purpose and contemplating life. People that are existential may include scientists, philosophers, or physicists. Socrates and Buddha are two very famous people that Gardener would note to have and exhibit an extremely high existential intelligence level.

6. <u>Interpersonal Intelligence (People Smart)</u>

Interpersonal intelligence is all about a person's ability to understand, relate and interact effectively with other people. They can naturally and easily pick up on people's moods and feelings and are more aware of non-verbal nuances and behaviors. Some famous people considered to be high in interpersonal intelligence would be Mahatma Gandhi, Mother Theresa, Ronald Reagan, and Eleanor Roosevelt.

7. <u>Intrapersonal Intelligence (Self Smart)</u>

Intrapersonal intelligence is having the ability to reflect on your own progress and to self evaluate. Self-discipline and motivation is an attribute, and the ability to work independently. Many people that are high in intrapersonal intelligence enjoy writing in journals and reflection, they have the ability to adjust and redirect as well as enjoy their alone time. It is also about how a person communicates within their own mind and their self-talk. Anne Frank is an example of a person with high intrapersonal intelligence, especially so as the journaling and writing she did were under incredibly difficult and challenging circumstances.

8. Bodily-Kinesthetic Intelligence (Body Smart)

Kinesthetic intelligence is having a high ability and level to be in tune with your body. Also, it includes the ability to move and perform with more flow agility. Examples of people that are highly kinesthetic are athletes, dancers, surgeons, people that are good with their hands and making or building things. Kinesthetic people learn well by the experience of doing something rather than watching or listening.

9. Spatial Intelligence (Picture Smart)

Spatial intelligence includes people that tend to be more visual and can picture images. They may seem to have a natural gift to be able to see things in their minds eye. These include people who enjoy painting and visual medium arts and people that are good at looking at pictures of charts and graphs and can interpret them. Designers would be considered having spatial intelligence because of having the ability to see in their mind how to create and use space.

Now that I have described what each intelligence embodies let's talk about how that comes into play in the workplace and why understanding the nine intelligences can be very beneficial.

Imagine being in a work environment, and your primary job is dealing with customer service issues, but your real strength is mathematical and numbers. You can do your job okay, but what really excites you is also being able to help calculate data and ways to track and improve efficiency. You love looking at sales graphs and charts to look for customer patterns and trends. If a manager understands this concept, they can cultivate a person's other intelligences, which can be a great asset to the team in helping achieve goals. Awareness and openness to a person's other natural interests and talents is an approach and, when applied, can help people feel more value and contribution. Also, they are being included in not just the job they were hired for but also acknowledged for other areas they are really good at and that can help the team be more successful. This can prove to add a higher level of fulfillment and job satisfaction. Or imagine a work environment that is dull in appearance and in need of improvements, so people feel more comfortable and happy in the workspace. Someone with spatial intelligence would enjoy contributing to creating and improving the workspace or area and be naturally good at coming up with ideas.

Here is another scenario that may cause or contribute to tension due to very different types of intelligences that are coworkers sharing space. One person is inclined to work and focus better with soft music playing, but the other is sensitive to sounds and tones and finds even low or soft music distracting. These are just a few examples, but you can imagine how useful understanding and incorporating people's other intelligence and learning styles would help alleviate many problems between personalities.

Alleviating problems and building upon people's natural intelligences is a highly effective approach to creating more team synergy, understanding, and empathy instead of potential irritations and annoyance.

Chapter 5

A Look Into Personality Drivers

Understanding the importance of personality drivers and significant needs contributes to a better work culture as it cultivates an understanding of others' unique differences and natural tendencies. Just as understanding Gardener's concepts on honoring the nine types of intelligences, there is much benefit to understanding and incorporating training and development around people's different personalities, needs, and values. In my training programs, I like to incorporate a fun and interactive activity for the participants to really get a good understanding of what personality drivers are and how they come into play in a big way in the work environment as well as in any relationship. Incorporating a fun and interactive activity is an entertaining and effective way to improve team spirit and morale. It is also a way to break communication barriers and create better understanding between the individuals participating.

For more information on programs and workshops, I can be contacted at amber@workculturesolutions.com

It is common for companies to utilize many tests to determine if a person is a good match for a position, such as the Meyers Briggs, Disc, and Caliper personality tests. A few years ago I had the opportunity to do a training focused on the significance of personality drivers with Robert Harrison who runs a very successful business in the bay area of California. He is also the training director of <u>NLPCA.com</u>. Mr. Harrison over his many years working and coaching people had developed an excellent program to help people better understand themselves. I felt so strongly about the impact this would have on helping people interact with their communication that I incorporated his training into my programs. What I have found very effective in coaching teams is to create an awareness of personalities and the role they play in how well people get along. If personality tests are used to help understand individuals' strengths and opportunities for improvement, a team's performance can be significantly improved. The following scenario is an example.

Connie walked into the office a few minutes after 8:00 a.m., looking a bit frazzled and rushed. It was fairly common for Connie to be rushing in; she was rarely on time. Connie was a single parent with two small children and also working her way through graduate school. She had been with this company for a couple of years, and the relationship with a few of her teammates always seemed strained. Connie felt she was trying really hard to get along with everyone and was always polite, offering to do additional work to take more of the team's load. Jane was Connie's manager and had been with the company since graduating from high school. She had been promoted several times and was now managing a team of ten. Several members of Jane's team had complained that Connie was continuously late. There was frustration that Connie did not keep up with documenting her workflow process. As a manager, Jane was very adamant about the team documenting their workflow process and keeping a shared database current. This ensured everyone could follow a project or step in if someone was absent. Jane had spoken to Connie about the importance of keeping her work process current, but Connie still seemed to let it slide. Jane also recognized that Connie was able to accomplish a lot during the workday, almost the work of two people. She was quick to pick up a project and run with it and manage several projects at once. Jane was not sure what to do as she valued Connie's flexibility and great attitude, always offering to take on more. On the other hand, the other team members had valid complaints; it was creating noticeable tension within the department. Jane decided to seek support outside of the department to find a solution.

In this situation, it is apparent that Connie's personality and style require little supervision, and she is very competent in taking on many projects and getting them done. However, it also shows that Connie's strength is not around detail and documentation. She enjoys and thrives on having multiple tasks and responsibilities, and although the work is quality, she is challenged in an area important to her manager and team. Connie's personality needs are rooted in wanting to do things as she wants and not be managed throughout the process. She likes taking on multiple tasks to have options for different things on which to work. This is her naturally driven style; it is neither right nor wrong. If personality differences were discussed when training with the team, it would have prevented much frustration and resentment.

Knowing how team members work best and building upon strengths openly makes it okay for people to build upon their individual strengths. It also provides an opportunity to discuss how to co-create an atmosphere based on transparency. We are better at some things and more challenged in certain areas. This approach allows people to know each other's strengths and use them to shift weaknesses rather than create a culture of judgment and frustration. People can also be tasked with workloads in a way that takes advantage of how the team can perform optimally.

Perhaps another team member really enjoys data entry and is excellent at documenting workflow. Bringing out individual strengths and preferences helps balance work and increase productivity while acknowledging people's different styles and personalities. This naturally impacts the well-being of employees.

To help further understand this, let's look at people's significant needs, personality drivers, and values. I will break it down into five distinct personality types and describe the benefits and challenges.

When a person becomes more aware of how they are

naturally driven and shares this with other people, it opens up communication, understanding, and empathy. We are all naturally wired, like the nine types of intelligences to a certain extent. When we find areas in our life that fulfill this natural gravitation, life is more fulfilling and rewarding because we are doing something that we feel in sync with. Here is a description of five different personality drivers that was developed by Robert Harrison's work:

Personality Driver Descriptions:

Freedom:	• Loves options • Requires little guidance • Not a fan of rules.
Security:	• Prefers the safest route. • Always looking for the most secure way. • Can be defensive as a way to stay in a comfort zone. • Likes routine.
Belonging:	• Loves to be part of a team. • Feels best with a group or being a member. • Goes with the flow of the group or team. • Conforms as just likes to be included.
Self Expression:	• The feeling of being different and unique is important. • Tends to stand out in a crowd. • Feels that what works for most people will work for them.
Competency:	• It is important that they are thought or perceived as smart. • Loves and takes pride in solving problems. • A driving need to prove themselves.

Personality Driver Strengths:

Freedom:	• Risk taker, likes challenges and is self motivated. • Thinks outside the box. • Needs little management
Security:	• Follows rules to a T. • Can do the same routine without getting bored • Stays at a job for a longtime and be satisfied.
Belonging:	• Great team attitude and player • Takes others into consideration and follows the rules • Has the back of the team.
Self Expression:	• Always coming up with new ideas. • Likes to flow freely without needing structure. • Has no problem speaking up. • Often a very creative person.
Competency:	• Hardworking and a lot of tenacity to succeed. • Loves being challenged and prefers to lead others. • Shows much confidence.

Personality Driver Challenges:

Freedom:	• Difficulty following rules. • Will interrupt a process if they feel it's necessary. • Resists long commitments.
Security:	• Any chaos is difficult to manage. • Loves structure and process. • Resistant to change of routines.
Belonging:	• Needs validation from others around decisions. • Does not challenge norms or think out of the box. • Finds it hard to work alone.
Self Expression:	• Can be easily distracted. • Always needing to stand out or speak up and be different. • Many times thinking of self first.
Competency:	• A tendency to always have to be right. • Likes to make things their own way. • Being part of a team can be difficult as they are inclined to want to lead.

From these charts, you can easily see how understanding and bringing this awareness into a group or team of people working together would better help the overall departmental function. It also improves an individual's awareness of their natural strengths and areas that they can develop that would help them feel more confident in themselves and specific situations. For example, imagine you are a person that is naturally driven to love freedom and options. It just appeals to you, and you are happiest in life when you have lots of choices and can work at your own pace. If you understand this about yourself, you are able to know what might be a better fit for you in your personal and professional life. However, knowing your challenges opens up opportunities for you to grow and move forward in certain areas.

I can relate to a person who prefers freedom, a *freedom person*. I love working for myself and having my own schedule. I love working on the things I like, and structure is a challenge for me because it feels limiting. Since I know this, I also understand that I must implement structure and schedule time for things that support my business, such as marketing, website maintenance, calendar management, and other administrative functions for my business to continue to grow and excel.

Now imagine a scenario where you have a team of people, and you have various personalities. This could create a lot of headaches. The freedom person might be annoyed with the security-based person and think they are not flexible. The security person may feel uncomfortable with the freedom person's approach to work and lack of needing structure. Freedom people go through life looking for options, and if they do not have them, they feel boxed in and uncomfortable. A security person goes through life, looking for safety and routine. Without that, they feel uncomfortable and lack certainty and security. If these different drivers were understood, the team members could work to complement each other and learn from each other. Bringing this type of training into any team setting is a total game-changer for facilitating positive behavior and improving the culture. Applying this information to your personal life will help you communicate better with family and friends. Here is a way to utilize this exercise in team building.

TEAM BUILDING EXERCISE:

1. Explain the different personality drivers to the group.

2. Have individuals write down privately what their top two drivers are.

3. Have the group write down privately on a separate sheet of paper what the top two drivers are for their teammates.

4. Gather the information and tabulate the group's understanding of one another.

5. Have a discussion about the group's perception and then discuss individually how each group member perceives themselves.

This is an excellent exercise to bring about understanding and help people to feel more comfortable in their natural styles. Then a conversation can begin regarding how this information can be useful in working together as a team. I have facilitated this team-building exercise many times, and the results were transformational. It opened up a whole new perspective about people's natural talents and strengths as well as opportunities to improve other areas. Also, it opened up opportunities for people to share and support tasks in a more cohesive and productive way.

For more information and training materials contact:

www.workculturesolutions.com

Chapter 6

Five Behaviors to Improve Work, Life, and Well-being

In this chapter, I will talk about *five always behaviors* that,

when embraced, instantly help a person gain rapport with others and foster better outcomes. The definition of rapport is: "relation, connection, especially harmonious or sympathetic relation." Rapport also embodies words like empathy, sympathy, affinity, harmony, compatibility, togetherness, interrelationship, relationship, concord, agreement, soul, unity, link, cotton, groove, bond, sympatico. Imagine simple behaviors that result in all the above?

These five steps provide a foundation or framework for setting the *tone* of your communication, which directly affects your company and team's mood and atmosphere. When used internally or with clients, customers, or patients, these behaviors will foster a first great impression and instill a sense of connection. When they are also used in everyday life, they facilitate a positive and immediate experience with the other person. Typically, when people meet for the first time or in a new setting, it is common for them to feel nervous, anxious, and even vulnerable. Following these steps, no matter what role you are in, helps to naturally address these feelings through a process that satisfies an emotional component.

The behaviors I will discuss in this chapter also convey respect upon meeting; they are good behaviors and good manners. When I think about these, I think about the saying "mind your manners." These behaviors are also evidence-based, meaning they have been studied and proven to increase patient relationships in the medical field. The well-known Beryl Clinic and Cleveland Clinic, and other best-in-class hospitals, have incorporated these behaviors into their culture and measured the behaviors to national benchmarks for patient experience. They have instilled these *always behaviors* and have shown to have increased patient satisfaction measurements significantly. We can apply these behaviors to any business because they are just plain good and considerate ways of being. Let's take a look at them.

1. Always Acknowledge and the 10/5 Rule: This is a way of greeting people whether or not you know them. The 10/5 rule is to make eye contact at 10 feet and smile; at five feet, greet the person. Attitude is everything, and people take cues from your attitude. The first impression is a lasting one, so this is a huge opportunity to set the tone. Here is an example:

"Good morning/afternoon Mr. Smith," or if on a first name basis, use the person's name.

People naturally feel more engaged when their name is used; it instantly becomes more personal. You can add to this by saying, "Great to meet you" or "How are you doing today?"

A few years ago, I flew to the west coast for business and had a layover in Chicago. My flight got delayed because of weather conditions, and it was going to prevent me from making my next connection. I know this scenario is not new to people who travel a lot; however, it is still filled with much stress and upset for many. I got referred to a line of people that were all waiting to get rerouted. People in front of me were all pretty upset, and some straight-up angry. As I was standing there, I decided not to get emotional about the situation as it was out of my control and just observe other people's reactions. As I stood there and observed how people were reacting and interacting with the ticket agent who was really trying to help, it was horrible to watch the level of anger and distress. People were not self-regulating, and the poor agent was taking a ton of grief from customers. The ticket agent looked absolutely exhausted and frazzled. When my turn came, as I approached her, I could tell she was bracing herself for another upset customer and preparing to be yelled at. I noticed her name on her name tag right away, and when I walked up, I said, "Hi Nathalie, my name is Amber, and I really appreciate you trying to help me out today." Her demeanor instantly changed as she took my ticket to help me rebook; she softened, smiled, seemed to relax her body a bit, and thanked me. I continued to chat about the situation, acknowledging her and how great she was doing under pressure. Long story short, Nathalie went above and beyond to find me another more direct flight. The exchange felt good as we did not project anything negative towards one another, just simply acknowledged and respected each other.

2. <u>Always Introduce Yourself</u>: When you are meeting someone for the first time, whether it is an internal employee or an external person, say your name. Depending on the circumstance, you could ask if they need directions or if you can help direct them.

This is a polite gesture and adds to the connection. Here is an example:

"Good morning Mr. Smith; how are you doing today?" "My name is Bill. Great to meet you."

"Do you need any help or direction to get where you're going today?" OR

"I have been expecting you and am ready for our meeting today."

3. <u>Always Speak Highly of Yourself and Your Coworkers</u>: Speaking highly of yourself, or a coworker is called managing up. This is a very important behavior as it lends credibility to you and your teammates. When you are working with a client or patient, it is important to manage yourself up and your coworkers. You can say things such as, "I love this field and enjoy helping others succeed." Or, "I

always wanted to work in this field, which I find so fulfilling." You can also mention your team and comment on how dedicated they are and passionate about what they do. Or you can make a positive statement about a particular person with whom they may be working.

Think of ways you can speak highly of yourself and your coworkers in your interactions. Incorporating this behavior and making these comments helps the other person feel at ease and gives them more confidence in the service you are providing and the entire team. You can also incorporate your organization and make a positive statement about it or its mission. When any service is being offered or provided, people naturally want to feel good about who they are working with or with whom they are doing business. This behavior accomplishes this as well as establishes a deeper connection with the other person. It also affects your team when they hear you managing up which means that you are speaking highly of them as well as creates good feelings and confidence in what service is being provided. Imagine a time you have been in a situation where a person complimented you to another or spoke about you in high regard. It felt good, didn't it? Manage up as much as you can; it makes you feel good because it is a positive action that evokes a positive feeling for both your coworker and the person you are providing or offering to a service to. Customers, clients, and patients will feel more comfortable with the service you provide when a sense of confidence is conveyed.

4. Always Listen: There is a big difference between

listening and hearing. When you are truly listening to someone, you are with them and not listening to the voices in your head. Being present when someone is talking and making eye contact is a very powerful way to get in sync with the other person. It conveys that you respect them and are truly interested. When you are listening and present, you are also more likely to pick up on other subtle nuances, such as tone, pitch, or information that you may miss if you think of other things. This can be challenging as human beings are wired to think of many different things at once. Have you ever been in a conversation and knew that person was somewhere else? I have too many times to count, and it instantly changed how I felt about engaging with the person. I have also done this many times – not been truly listening –and when I catch myself, I bring my attention right back to the person. Or have you ever had the experience of thinking about how to respond before the person was finished talking? How can anyone possibly be listening when you are already thinking about how to respond? Have you ever experienced being in a conversation, and someone looks at their phone? It happens a lot. I understand that at times we have to do that as we may be waiting on an important call. Otherwise, though, it is just a habit when we are engaging with someone else as it interrupts the conversation and gives the impression that you're not listening, and that can break the rapport.

5. <u>Always Thank People and Express Gratitude</u>: This is a huge game-changer when you are interacting with

someone. A sincere thank you speaks volumes when you tell someone who is helping you that you appreciate their help. If you are running late, express gratitude for their patience, again acknowledging and validating through appreciation.

If you are in service to someone by helping them, caring for them, or training them, let them know you are happy to have the opportunity to help them in the way you are providing that service. Expressing gratitude to another person is an emotion when exchanged feels good to do and feels good to the other person. Here are some examples:

"Thank you so much for trusting me to be part of your project; I really enjoyed working with you."

"I am honored that you trust me to be a part of your care today."

"Thank you so much for your contribution to today's meeting; it was very helpful."

When I was working a few years ago as a physician's coach, I had the opportunity to observe doctors caring for their patients. One I particularly remember deeply resonated with me as it was very touching. This specific morning I was observing an emergency department doctor. She was relatively new to the organization, with lots of energy and excellent at putting her patients at ease right away. She used the five behaviors right out of the gate and was a natural at relating to patients.

The morning that I was observing her, I went into a

room where she was attending an elderly woman. I could tell that the patient was scared and felt very vulnerable. It had been established that she lived alone and did not have any family nearby. She had been having some irregular heartbeats and was getting a series of tests done. This emergency room doctor was very attentive to her and picked up on her vulnerability. She spoke to her in such a way that was calming and comforting. What resonated with me the most was that when the elderly lady was being discharged, the emergency room doctor took her hand in hers and looked at her very sincerely and said, "You're going to be just fine, and I want you to know how honored I am to have been able to care for you today. Thank you for trusting me." It was a powerful moment, and I got to witness it. The elderly lady was teary-eyed, and she thanked the doctor and told her how much it meant to her that she took the time and made her feel like she mattered. She went on to explain that in her experience, most people had left her feeling invisible.

Think about how powerful this moment of presence and exchange of gratitude impacted these two people. Well, three when you count me, the observer.

Imagine incorporating one or two of these behaviors and what a difference it would make in any environment. This is a genuine connection from a fundamental level of courtesy and respect from human being to human being through acknowledgment. This is a connection before whatever the activity is, the point of connection that most of us need and desire: to feel heard, valued, respected, and listened to make a defining difference for how we continue to relate in our everyday lives. We are composed of emotions, and that emotion creates energy within us and our surroundings, which directly impacts our day to day life.

Chapter 7

Four Good Behaviors For Bad Situations

In this chapter, I am going to go over behaviors to live by when presented with a challenging situation. When you incorporate these behaviors as a proactive strategy to address customer or client service issues, you will have a much better chance of improving the situation's outcome.

Let's face it, things do not always go as planned in life. When you are interacting with other people and face a situation that did not go as expected it can throw people off, and emotions can get charged. It is important to have a proactive approach to situations that occur that are unexpected or take a different direction, which may not be desirable. Examples of these situations could be a meeting postponed, an appointment running behind schedule, someone is late to a meeting, a vacation delay, covering someone's responsibilities if they are ill.

Think about a time when you have had a bad or even horrible customer service experience and how it may have frustrated you. If that experience left you feeling like the person delivering the service did not respond to your experience in a way that satisfied you, you may have found yourself getting even more upset and frustrated.

Think of another time when you had the same experience, perhaps at a restaurant when your food was served cold or your order got mixed up. How did the wait staff handle this for you? If you're like me, you have had bad experiences handled horribly and bad experiences dealt with well. Things happen all the time that are out of our control, but how we respond to them makes a huge difference when interacting with people or providing a service.

I had just purchased a new vehicle and was getting used to the new navigation systems and computerized things the car could do. I loved that it was considered a very safe car as I traveled a lot and through winters with no shortage of snow and ice. This vehicle was a bit to get used to, and there was a learning curve to how it operated. I had it for about one month, came out to start it one morning, and it would not start. It would not turn over; not a sound, just dead. I had to call a tow company to jump-start the battery. It was a bit irritating because I had an appointment a few hours away, and this set me back. I figured that I would get the battery checked, and that would solve the problem. When I took it in for service, I was told the battery was fine and that it was strange what had happened. It happened several more times, and I began to get very irritated as I was not getting the support I felt I should from the dealership. The final time it happened, I had my car towed to the service center, extremely upset because I was now stranded. I walked into the service department already very upset about the car and also very ready to let the service manager know. I will never forget the young man that was working that day. Within minutes, he had completely turned the situation around because he did some essential things right out of the gate. These behaviors will be explained a little later in the chapter. In the end, I found out I did not realize that I had been leaving my car in auto mode, which was draining the battery.

Life does not always go as planned, and when things do not, and you are involved in calming the situation down, here are four behaviors that will help to diffuse things:

1. Acknowledge the Situation: To the other person or people involved will validate what happened; simple acknowledgment goes a long way to starting to diffuse a situation. Saying something like this will make a noticeable positive difference. People naturally want and like to be validated.

   "I know this is frustrating for you," or "I can only imagine how difficult this is," and you could add also add "my sincere apologies that this has happened."

2. Always be transparent and honest about what

occurred: The young man that helped me that day with my car told me that the car I had could be very complicated and not obvious about certain features. Explaining this to me helped me with my frustration level and let me know that this model caused the same problem for other people. He also went on to say that it should have been pointed out to me. If a situation occurs when you are delivering changing news, you can always offer an appropriate explanation. For example, if you run late to an appointment or meeting, acknowledge it, and then give a brief explanation. When I spoke earlier about the restaurant scenario and being delivered cold or the wrong food had the wait-staff said something like, "I am so sorry that happened. I made a mistake and did not realize your order was ready." Or, "I mixed up your table and will take care of this right away," in doing this, it demonstrates transparency, honesty, and also the person is taking responsibility.

3. Offer an option or options for the situation: This is important as people like to have options instead of being told that this is just the way it is. An example of this is to offer new times to reschedule a meeting or offering someone who is waiting some water or a coffee. These are small examples, but they make a huge difference as the person feels respected as well as their time valued.

4. Offer an apology or express empathy for the situation. Any time I have been in a situation that

went wrong, or I had to wait if the person apologized to me and expressed that they were sorry for the change and the interruption to my schedule, it made a huge difference. A sincere apology goes a long way to improving the outcome in an upsetting situation and how you and the company you are representing are perceived.

When I have been in a situation where I have had to change a plan with someone or deliver difficult news, I always offer these four steps. Things do not always go perfectly, but when someone is treated with acknowledgment, honesty, options, and empathy, they are less likely to be upset or stay upset. It also will make a difference in how they speak about you or your business to other people.

Think about how applying these behaviors in any professional setting within customer service would improve relations. These behaviors are provide a solid strategy that is creating a proactive approach to challenging situations, and that is a solid plan if you are in any business that involves people. It can result in retaining a customer or employee instead of losing them. It can result in the difference between someone speaking ill of your company or business to other people, which directly affects your image and credibility. If you go beyond this individual interaction and think of corporate or global accounts and clients that you may service, these behaviors are a must to follow and incredibly important to embrace as a strategy for service recovery. Most people will be much more understanding and cooperative if they are offered these four behaviors based on values of respect for the other party.

In the medical field, when things go wrong, it can lead to dire consequences.

After all, it is the profession that is all about people's health as well as life and death. No one is perfect, and unfortunately, sometimes things do go wrong, and good outcomes are compromised; it happens and is part of life. However, the research shows that if people are treated kindly, validated, and shown respect and empathy, they are far less likely to complain or go beyond that to file grievances or seek litigation.

There are countless varieties of situations in life that change. Depending on the person's personality and threshold to handle changes, it can challenge people to effectively regulate their emotions. Naturally, some people are better at managing how they respond and able to be more flexible around changing circumstances. However, a proactive approach to a changing or upsetting situation can be dramatically improved by a methodical approach to the situation.

As you reflect on this chapter, consider times you were in a position requiring you to deliver bad news or communicate a significant change of plans in the schedule. Or think of a time that you were on the receiving end. What was your experience? What difference would it have made if these behaviors were exhibited? Although you may not have liked the situation, you would likely have felt better about how it had been handled because somebody considered you. If you were in the situation of being the one to deliver unpleasant news or changes, having a proactive four-step approach would help alleviate the stress of the situation.

When I walked out of that car dealership that day, I went from being very upset to feeling utterly calm because of how it was handled.

Chapter 8

Beyond Voice Behavior's

People tend to like people that like them because it makes them feel more comfortable. Behaviors go far beyond words when relating to other people and getting in rapport with them. In chapter six, I discussed the definition of rapport and its importance in influencing positive outcomes. In essence, rapport is a way of behaving. Communication is so much more than the words we choose to speak. Non-verbal communication, according to some research, has far more of an impact on how well the relationship begins and develops. The words you choose are important, but the nuances you attach with that communication is sending information to the other person that can significantly influence how that conversation goes.

In my training, which is behavior-based communication styles, the *structure of communication* is broken down into categories or influencers. I believe because of all of the extensive training, observations, and clients, I have seen that this structure is valid and applicable. As you continue with this chapter, you will understand why.

Here are how the communication structure works and the influence categories. I am sure there are more, but this covers most.

WORDS

TONALITY

PHYSIOLOGY

The essence of rapport with someone is essential that when we are similar to each other, there is a tendency to like each other. When you can learn how to get in rapport with someone, you gain responsiveness with each other in the conversation. Why is this so important? When a person is comfortable with you, they are more likely to respond to you, trust you, listen to you, and be open to what you say. If something along the way does not go well, having established good rapport will be extremely beneficial for how that person moves on with you. Imagine how beneficial these behaviors would be when working with teammates, clients, patients, and anyone in your personal life.

Let's break down the influence categories to get a better understanding and feeling for what nuances and elements are of those. Once you get familiar with these, you can start to incorporate them into your conversations and notice what a difference they make when you become aware. As you continue reading, I will give you examples of how to incorporate these into your communication style.

PHYSIOLOGY	TONALITY	WORDS
✔ Posture, proximity	✔ Tone(pitch)	✔ Predicates
✔ Gestures	✔ Speed (tempo)	✔ Key words
✔ Facial expressions	✔ Timbre (quality)	✔ Common experiences
✔ Breathing	✔ Volume (loudness)	✔ Contents or hierarchy of thoughts and ideas, i.e., big picture or details

Learning these influencers creates something called a matching/mirroring experience with the other person, which creates rapport. The chart above gives you ways of what to incorporate under each category. Here are some examples for you to practice how to use these non-verbal behaviors to create rapport instantly:

Start by observing the person. What do you see?

Posture and Proximity: Are they standing straight or hunched with shoulders forward?

How close do they stand to another person (depending on the situation or environment) if possible to observe?

Do they cross their arms together when talking?

Do they cross their legs?

Do they tap their fingers or feet?

Do they keep their hands in their pockets or let them hang by their side?

What gestures are they using? Gestures are forms of non-verbal communication, which are movements of the hands, arms, legs, and face. Here are some examples:

Pointing

Leaning in

Making an okay sign

Making a thumbs up

Making a fist

Rubbing their hands

Eye rolling

Raising their arms in the air

Putting a hand on their chest area

Extremely important to be aware of concerning gestures. Concerning gestures are gestures that in one culture do not mean the same thing in another. This is a great opportunity to become aware of diversity and respect for other cultures, races, and religions.

For example:

Making the okay sign with your hand in the US and UK means something is acceptable. However, in Japan, it means money; in Brazil, it is an insult; it means a zero in Russia.

Crossing fingers while in the US is a sign of luck; it is like giving someone the middle finger and is considered vulgar in Vietnam.

Thumbs up in the US, this is a sign of support and camaraderie, but for anyone that's cultural influence are countries such as West Africa and the Middle East, it is as offensive as pointing a middle finger at someone in the US.

Some of these gestures we naturally do in communicating, and these are all non- verbal. Still, if we are aware that there may be other implications, we can prevent a potentially uncomfortable situation.

Facial expressions:

Observe if their expression is strained, smiling, or frowning, and notice how it changes within the conversation. If you are watching closely, you can pick up non- verbal cues as to their mood, personality, and how they are feeling. Upon meeting someone, either for the first time or whether you have met a person before, you can instantly gauge their mood or state by observing their facial expression. By observing, you can match it or mismatch it to what they are saying, depending on the situation. I will go into matching and mirroring later in this chapter.

Breathing:

Noticing someone's breathing can give you valuable insight into how a person is feeling, which helps give you information on how you might respond and speak with them. If someone is breathing quickly, it may mean they are nervous or anxious. It could also indicate a possible health issue if you notice wheezing or labored breathing. It might seem odd to notice breathing, but it is non-verbal information that can clue you into how a person is feeling, and being aware gives you an advantage in your approach with them.

Tonality and pitch:

What do you hear? Does the person use a lot of variance in how high or low their voice is? Does it change depending on what they are saying? Do they talk very fast or slowly, and do they pronounce words clearly? Do you notice any accent or dialect?

Imagine just noticing these, and as you become more aware, you can get a feeling for how high or low their energy level is. You can also get a feel for what excites them if their voice gets higher or speeds up. If when their voice drops, you may notice it could be around something they take seriously or are reflecting on. Again it is information and data to help you get into rapport with that person.

A good friend of mine told me that she and her colleagues noticed when her boss was feeling stressed because his tone, pitch, and volume increased, and he started talking faster. He would also get noticeably red or flushed in his neck and face area.

Words:

Nouns, verbs, keywords, and descriptions tell you

how a person relates to life. Notice what words are being used and ones that are used frequently. Another important aspect to notice if a person likes to share stories or experiences. This is an excellent way to relate to someone or something. How does this person categorize the content of their words, meaning do they use lots of detail, or are they more of a higher overview, big picture person? When speaking with a person that has more of a big picture frame of mind, going into too much detail can lose them or overwhelm them.

Let's talk about how you know if you are in rapport or gaining rapport with someone after you have become aware of the non-verbal communication influencers. Here are four indicators that you will begin to notice. The last one I list is the most compelling indicator that you're really in sync with the person, which is auditory digital.

All human beings have ways that they process information by a preferred representational system. There are four primary systems that can tell you a lot about someone. This does not mean that they are just one, but frequently one is stronger than the other. When you can notice these nuances, what naturally happens is that it allows you to communicate back in a very similar way to how that person talks to themselves.

Below are the four primary ways that people process information, and also the indicators of whether you are in rapport with them. The primary are: visual, auditory (and auditory digital), and kinesthetic (or the VAK system). Again these are not the only ones, but they are the primary representational systems.

VISUAL:

People that are visual are generally well-groomed and neat; they tend to keep their heads and eyes up. They have a tendency to memorize things in images or pictures. They are interested in how things look and appear. They can be challenged by remembering instructions but do well with being shown. In conversations, you may notice the use of *seeing* words such as:

I get the picture.

I can see that clearly.

That looks good to me.

Here are some other visual words: look, view, appears, show, envision, foggy, focused, show.

INDICATORS FOR VISUAL:

An indicator to know if you are establishing rapport with a visual person is that you will feel a color shift in yourself (such as a flushed feeling in your face) and then notice it in the other person. It may also be noticed in a change from a lighter tone to darker depending on how the person relaxes their face. Nervousness can cause redness or flush in a person's face, cheeks, neck, or a blotchy red appearance. You will notice that change will fade as the person becomes more comfortable with you and more in rapport.

AUDITORY:

People that have a favored auditory representational system may talk to themselves. Their eyes may move from side to side in conversation. They are easily distracted by noises. They can repeat things back to you and have an easy time learning from listening. They enjoy listening to music and talking on the phone and also respond to certain tones and words. An auditory person is interested in hearing what you have to say.

INDICATOR FOR AUDITORY:

You can tell if you are in rapport with an auditory person as they might say to you things to you like:

Have we met before? Do I know you?

I feel like I have known you for years!

Auditory people may also use words like this:

I hear you!

That sounds great!

I like the way that sounds!

I did not like the tone of that meeting.

Some additional auditory cues/words: hear, listen, in tune, all ears, rings a bell, resonate and harmonize.

KINESTHETIC:

People tend to get closer to you when they are talking. They also move and talk more slowly and methodically. They enjoy physical rewards and also are comfortable with touch, such as a handshake or a pat on the shoulder. They are focused on how things feel to them and what feels right.

Some phrases a kinesthetic person may use are:

That feels right to me.

I got the feeling that you were going to do that. Something was off with that meeting.

I have a hunch that we need to go in a different direction.

Some additional kinesthetic words/cues: hard, concrete, get a grip, grasp, catch on, tap into.

INDICATORS OF KINESTHETIC:

You may experience a kindred feeling or warmth from the other person.

You may notice the person feeling comfortable to be in a close space with you or tend to reach out towards you while talking.

AUDITORY DIGITAL:

People that are auditory digital spend a lot of time talking to themselves. They have other characteristics of the other three systems as this one is derived from those. When you are talking with someone who is thinking about what you are saying, they usually look to the right or left, meaning they are having a self-dialogue.

MIRRORING AND MATCHING:

I want to go into a few other non-verbal behaviors that I have touched on already in the digital auditory description, which is called matching and mirroring behavior:

Within the concept of rapport, mirroring and matching is creating a state that both people are responding to one another. When a person starts to follow your lead more, this is a sure indicator that they are in rapport with you. You can test this by shifting your posture, crossing your legs, or putting your hand on your chin. Pick up a glass or move an object and watch to see if they mimic that. Cross a leg, and notice if they cross their leg or perhaps the opposite one. If you lean in, do they lean in? You can test this in multiple ways.

Now that we have gone over these non-verbal behaviors, you can begin to see, imagine and understand the impact of body language and the importance of becoming aware of it for yourself and while observing other people.

As you become more aware of these nuances, you can start to observe and incorporate body language awareness into your communication and interactions. This will instantly get you in rapport and sync with the other person. Mirroring and matching, is intended to create a feeling of likeness and relatability. If the other person is standing at a distance, respect the space. If they talk a lot with their hands, use yours. If they speak slowly, mirror that. If they speak louder, mirror that. If they make eye contact, match theirs. Notice what words they choose and use those words to relate and choose similar ones. Do you get the picture?

CROSS MATCHING BEHAVIOR:

Other ways of creating non-verbal rapport are to

cross-match a person. An example would be matching one part of your body with another, such as if the person folds their arms, you can cross a leg. If you notice the rhythm of someone's breathing, you could tap your finger at the same pace, and it sends off a non-verbal cue that you are in sync.

Matching and mirroring, and crossover matching are intended to be subtle so that the person you are with is not obvious to it. Although subtle, they do influence the energy exchange between the two people.

When I was working in corporate sales, I was visiting a large account that had some difficulties with the company I was working for. The vendor company, my employer, was going through some growing pains and technology updates.

Unfortunately, for a few of my accounts, these changes frustrated them as the service and delivery of products was a bit slower than usual. This put the account in a tense situation with their customers as they had to keep explaining and putting out fires. This was not the first time the vendor company had growing pains that spilled over onto accounts, but this particular account was a long-standing one and had been through a few changes with the vendor company I was representing. Many of the managers for this account had been there a long time and were becoming impatient in dealing with the change by the vendor company. My objective was to meet and hopefully facilitate some service recovery. I had a plan for the meeting based on the behaviors covered in chapters six and seven as my go-to strategy. While walking in feeling prepared, I will admit that I was a bit nervous. I went into the meeting room a little early to get set up and distribute the materials for the attendees. In this meeting, the attendees included everyone that worked in the office and impacted by the issues of the vendor company's growth changes. Those changes had affected their clients, and I was there to help them address that. There were about twenty-five people in the room, and things started out fairly well. People were frustrated with good reason but were open to listening. The strategy of behaviors based on the four cornerstones of acknowledging/ validating the situation, respect for the time involved, patience, offering options, and expressing empathy and gratitude worked very well at calming and addressing the frustrations and concerns. Subsequently, as I was almost finished, the vice-president of the company entered the room, arriving late from another meeting, and stood in the doorway. I greeted him, and right away, he went into a tailspin of frustration, expressing how tired he was that my company was unprepared and its effect on his business. He felt all he got was excuses. He went on to state that his reputation with his clients was being strained and demanded what was I going to do about it? Wow, talk about a bit uncomfortable. Everyone in the room was so silent you could hear a pin drop, and you can bet that all eyes were on me. I had to think quickly, and so I made a decision to match and mirror his emotion. I responded with the same mannerisms, raised my voice to his tone, pitch, cadence, and said, "I know! I 100% agree with you, and I can hear and see how frustrated you are and feeling like you're not getting the support you need." The way that I said this non-verbally was what made a difference.

He had been very charged and my choosing this approach to copy his mannerisms or match and mirror, I spoke his language, and he felt that I really understood. I went on to say that his level of upset showed how much he cared about the level of service to his clients and that this was part of the reason that his company had been so successful. By including and applying body language behavior, the vice-president instantly felt heard and calmed down, opening up to listen to me and the options and solutions I offered. He felt heard, validated and understood.

The lesson in this story is, as we know in life, things do not always go smoothly. However, what can make all the difference is being aware, observing, listening, showing respect and empathy, as well as attending to non-verbal behavior and cues. Imagine incorporating the awareness of your non-verbal communication with the people you are in contact with every day professionally and personally. Can you imagine now what a different experience that would create?

Chapter 9

The S.C.O.R.E Method For Group Facilitation

Turning challenges into opportunities

Bringing a group together to a common goal can be

challenging as it introduces many different opinions and perspectives. Everyone brings their own experiences and reference points to the table; this can cause divisiveness if not effectively facilitated.

Have you ever been in a meeting with a group trying to come up with a solution and walked out frustrated and throwing your hands in the air? I sure have, and I have seen it happen many times.

Taking into consideration each individual's contributions within a group is extremely important to the collaboration and congruency of the group. Facilitating within groups regarding new processes, adjustments to workflow, learning new services, and how it all interrelates and affects the people involved are common types of scenarios that require a facilitation strategy. People involved in group meetings typically work in different departments, but their work affects one another. This indirect relationship can lead to a lack of understanding if transparency is not created when working toward a common goal.

In my coaching career, I saw a pattern of communication in groups that would end in people disagreeing with one another and becoming disengaged or frustrated. I have also been part of group meetings that have gone off the rails and left everyone feeling more of a divide amongst the team. Having a systematic approach helps significantly reduce the conflict that might arise from the different variables in a group setting and keep behaviors positive.

Along with drawing from the behaviors already spoken about in the previous chapters, I developed a step-by-step method to have a productive group meeting when something needs to be facilitated. It gives each individual a chance to express themselves, share information, contribute, and collectively decide on the best option.

This method is effective, and it brings out the strengths of individuals and departments and opens up opportunities for growth based on the reality of available resources. It can also turn judgment into opportunities to move forward and create a better understanding of each other's individual responsibilities as well as departments and how they can better work together.

Here are the steps of how the method works:

Make sure to use a whiteboard as a visual representation and document to keep track of the information. It can be used for follow up meetings and measuring progress towards the goal or goals established.

S - State the situation or overview: Weigh in on everyone's perspective and get an agreement from everyone's input as to what the situation is, then define it, and write it down. Make sure that before you move on, everyone feels good about the situation being addressed and how it is summarized.

C - Challenges: Write down the challenges the group is facing regarding the situation. Weigh in with everyone in the group. This is very important to get feedback and insight from everyone attending that is part of the process. Make sure everyone agrees and write them down. When people work in different departments, they are often unaware of the challenges that they may create for others or the challenges that exist outside of their own area of focus. This lack of awareness can lead to misinformation and misunderstanding. This step gives everyone a chance to learn more about how different departments function. When you bring people together, it widens the ability to effect better outcomes through shared knowledge.

O - Opportunities: Write down the possibilities and positive results of addressing the situation or change for the desired goal. There are always silver linings; this is important because naturally, some people are uncomfortable with change and want to resist. Looking at the situation in a different light or reframing it by identifying what opportunities will be accomplished by achieving this goal will help people look at the positive aspects of the goal rather than focus on the discomfort of change. Get feedback from everyone and congruence or agreement before moving forward. Write it down to document identified opportunities.

R - <u>Resources</u>: Have the group stay in the reality of what resources they can access to facilitate the situation or change now. Many people will get hung up on what they do not have and what would make things easier to implement the change or improve a situation. Keeping everyone grounded in reality helps to move the process forward and not get stuck in a debate of *if only*. Write down the resources available and keep the group focused in the now.

E - <u>Execution, plan to implement, and follow up</u>: Everyone contributes on how to best implement the actions towards the goal such as: what will the flow be, timelines, what is everyone's part in taking responsibility for the execution of the change. Everyone in the group contributes and weighs in for the plan to move forward. Establish how the plan can be measured for progress and figure out collectively how everyone will know that the change/goal is moving forward. Write those steps down and also who is involved in what parts of the plan's execution. Include anyone that has volunteered to keep track of additional ways to contribute to the group. Write that down as well. Plan a time to follow up with the group and measure and or adjust the progress, and follow the method again to completion.

I was working as a coach for a large hospital group. One of my areas of focus was the emergency department and the departments that supported everything that happened there, such as admitting, rooming, scheduling, x-rays, and laboratory services. There was a big issue with getting timely results back from some of the departments involved, and in emergent care, time is of the utmost importance. This issue also led to low patient satisfaction scores. The goal of the emergency department and the hospital was to collectively improve those satisfaction scores. The staff was lean at the time, and many people were feeling overwhelmed and overworked. Morale was down, and the employees were getting edgy with one another and blaming this on the fact that they did not have sufficient resources to do their jobs properly.

Although the hospital was actively looking to hire, there was uncertainty when they would be back up to a more manageable workload and flow. The situation had to be improved, and everyone needed to come together to work out a plan to more efficiently and productively improve patient satisfaction scores. When people came into the meeting, the mood was very charged, and you could tell there was a defensive posture towards the task of improving the scores due to resentment around not enough resources.

I used the S.C.O.R.E. method to acknowledge the situation, validate it, and open up the dialogue to get ideas and more efficient ways of doing things. What was great is that by bringing everyone together and letting everyone contribute, people could gain an understanding of other departments they were less familiar with. This opened up communication, which helped create understanding and empathy. It also provided an opportunity for the group to come together collectively for a common goal. They were able to identify what they actually did have for resources and how to make those resources work for the group and the goal in a more efficient way. The meeting ended up going very well, not to say there were not a few tense moments but having a guideline to go by provided a strategy to keep focused on what needed to be accomplished. Measurements were set up to evaluate progress, and follow-up meetings were planned to get team feedback. This would determine what was working and what might need adjustment to keep moving forward towards the goal. It also would serve to foster the team's communication and improve their relationships and efficiency. The patient satisfaction scores went up noticeably within three months.

It is important to note that this process is a strategy that serves as a structure and format for groups but is useful for individuals working on smaller projects. Using this method can also introduce and explore the personality drivers and nine types of intelligences discussed in earlier chapters. Imagine how much more including and creating that awareness would enrich the group connection and understanding.

Chapter 10

A Systematic Approach To Change

How to incorporate standards of good behavior

As you know now, this book is not written from a technical skills point of view; it focuses on behaviors or soft skills. Up to this point, my intention for this book has been to build the case to make a positive work culture a priority and behaviors that support that overall goal. This may all sound simplistic, but a positive work environment will equate to happy or happier employees. The costs of incivility and stress to a company can wallop the bottom line, and the bigger picture is the effect on the well-being of the people. Throughout this book, the soft skills presented are all about creating an environment and culture of understanding and empathy, one that balances transactions with transformation. Transactions are obviously part of day-to-day business operations and how we go about our life; however, understanding how to incorporate transformative leadership will improve every other transaction. The importance and significance that leadership embraces making work culture a priority sets the tone for the whole organization, company, or business, no matter how large or small. This quote by Daniel Goleman, a pioneer in the field of emotional intelligence, is one that really sums it up:

"In a very real sense we have two minds, one that thinks and one that feels."

Daniel Goleman, *Emotional Intelligence: Why It Can Matter More Than IQ*

The definition of transactional and transformational leadership is:

- Transactional Leadership: Works within set established goals and organizational boundaries.

- Transformational Leadership: Focuses on motivating and engaging followers with a vision of the future.

To further illustrate the differences between transactional leadership and transformational leadership, the following chart may be helpful.

Transactional	— Clarifies issues and focuses on problem-solving; prefers and makes high use of cognitive knowledge primarily.
	— Attempts to fix what is broken.
	— Communicates strategy plan charts a strategy course and communicates it to the team.
	— Develops meeting agenda and conducts meetings according to this preset and pressing agenda; expects agreement.
	— Intentionally works to avoid or circumvent conflicts and to contain contradiction.
	— Asks: what is happening out there? What should I/we do?
	— Stays focused on what they perceive to be the best idea.
	— Builds alliances of interest.
Transformational	— Clarifies personal purpose and integrity through an ongoing inner journey; uses emotional, cognitive, spiritual, and experiential knowledge.
	— Listens and asks honest, open questions; collegial style; attends to relational aspects.
	— Applies appreciative inquiry; looking for what is going well and what is working.
	— Facilitates the emergence of strategy from the collective intelligence of the group.
	— Translates values into clear specific meeting practices that ensure everyone's participation and keeps egos in check.
	— Devotes time to bringing conflicts to light and addressing them; applies conflict resolution process.
	— Asks: What is happening in me? How are others experiencing it? What is trying to or needs to emerge?
	— The leader is able to hold different points of view and integrate complex, divergent ideas.
	— Builds trustworthy relationships.

Human beings thrive when they are connecting and communicating in a healthy way, and a positive environment fosters this type of connection. A person's work-life represents a big chunk of a person's time, which affects their quality of life at home.

Over the years, I have witnessed so much unnecessary suffering. That suffering could have been avoided if the concepts and behaviors in this book had been incorporated. When any environment is lacking or absent in good behaviors, respect, understanding, and empathy, it results in relationships deteriorating. Chronic negativity and a lack of civility also contribute to a further decline and raise barriers around communicating so that any potential for a positive outcome between the parties involved diminishes rapidly. Everything that happens in a person's work-life affects their home life. Our environment is one of the biggest influences on our health. As you continue reading this chapter, I will provide a template on how to begin to make workplace behaviors a priority and how it must be aligned to be successful. This is not to be taken lightly; as human beings, we are made of emotions, and respond to those emotions and when they are tended to and managed effectively we thrive.

I can assure you that embracing and using this behavior model consistently will positively impact internal and external communications. The benefits of learning, embracing, and embedding these behaviors as non-negotiable will be huge to any business's bottom line. I have found it incredibly common that the skills and behaviors I have pointed out in this book, referred to as *soft skills,* are dramatically overlooked. It does not matter your company's size. Applying soft skills will help any business be more successful.

When hiring and bringing new people into the company, it is important to have a clear message of the company's cultural expectations—having a training program that is part of bringing on new hires regarding how employees treat one another as well as the people they serve. Involving teams in the process of hiring into their departments is a transformational behavior. Everyone can contribute input around the person joining the team is a good fit.

I wrote about the Peter Principle in chapter three, stating that it is not uncommon that people are repeatedly hired and promoted based on how well they do their job's particular skill set, their level of education and experience, but not how well they tend to interact or their ability to manage those interactions with other team members, clients, patients or customers. This presents a huge opportunity on which to capitalize.

Teaching people how to treat other people, talk to other people, listen to other people, become self-aware, and learn to regulate their emotions has a significant ripple effect. Starting off the hiring process and keeping this in mind will alleviate possible future frustrations within the department and teams. Happy and content employees will directly impact your relationships with customers, clients, and patients and every facet of business and people's personal lives. The benefits are enormous in costs saved through retention, engagement, productivity, attention to detail, reduced error, and potential litigation, to name a few. If people are unhappy within a company, that company's customers suffer the consequences too. Everyone in the entire system, at every point of transition or interaction, can feel the burden.

As you continue reading this chapter, you will read about an overview of a proactive approach based on connecting authentically through behavioral skills that promote positive communication and a healthier work culture. Keep in mind it must start at the top; if not, it is hard to sustain as attitudes are contagious.

Beginning the process:

The process begins by shifting to a commitment to behavior standards and starts with everyone. Here is an overview of what I have found that works to get the process moving.

1. Establish a top-down commitment to behavior excellence and a senior leadership commitment. If a company has a governing body or board, include them as they directly influence the senior leadership.

2. Make non-negotiable behaviors and work culture one of the top strategic priorities for the entire system and provide experiential (meaning hands-on and interactive) behavior training for everyone.

3. Invest in professional coaching to roll out programs and deploy a Train-The- Trainer program. Train-The-Trainer is a framework for training potential instructors or subject matter experts within the organization to enable them to train other people in their organization. The expected outcome is that attendees learn the new knowledge or skill, and they will instruct further groups of people in the organization with programs across the system and all departments.

4. Senior leadership, managers, and directors need to listen, listen, and listen more with neutrality, curiosity, and deep and authentic respect to your teams.

5. Spend time with the people where the work is done, talk with them, ask questions, and again listen, get feedback, and be interested.

6. Include, inform, and educate everyone about behavior initiatives.

7. Develop training programs to coach, encourage, mentor, and support everyone around behavior standards and development.

8. Genuinely engage managers and their teams in the process of development and training.

9. Establish a culture of excellence, get feedback continuously on workplace culture. *Everyone* owns non-negotiable behaviors and is

accountable.

10. Establish a way to follow up that includes open feedback from everyone involved and a way to measure progress.

At the beginning of developing a complete organizational approach, a period of observation must occur. How can you know where to go if you are not sure where you are? Feedback from those observations will provide you with a good starting point before any training or implementation. The observation phase is critical to the process because it provides information and data about the current work culture and establishes opportunities to improve. The observer has a rare opportunity to spend quality time with the people doing the workday in and day out in various circumstances and situations.

Making behaviors part of the job and establishing standard work processes for behaviors is key so the model can be followed, duplicated, and learned. It creates a consistent standard of how things are done. The definition of standard work is a detailed definition of the current best practices for performing an activity or process.

According to Lean Six Sigma (well-known for developing standard work) is a method that relies on a collaborative team effort to improve performance by systematically removing waste and reducing variation. Lean Six Sigma not only reduces process defects and waste but also provides a framework for overall organizational culture change.

Standard work is documentation that contains instructions, useful graphics, and anything else necessary to ensure that work is done consistently no matter who does it.

Development of detailed guides, marketing, and communication materials with step by step instruction establishes a framework for a behavior coaching model. It will serve as a guidebook to be used for standard work. These materials will provide consistency for everyone involved so that the processes can be followed and duplicated. Standard work may seem strange around behaviors, but if you have a reliable process as a guide to observe, set goals, and train, it becomes a system.

Here is an example of the various components and steps to guide you through how this works. Remember, it does not matter how small or large your company is; this is a general guide and can be adapted accordingly. I intentionally made this guide a large approach, but it is easily scalable.

The important point is whether you have ten employees, hundreds or thousands, this system can be utilized.

A multi-level systematic approach and the process consists of these workshop and training topics:

Always Behaviors

Service Recovery

Values and Personalities Drivers

Understanding Body Language

Train-the-Trainer

Stress Reduction

Once you have an organizational chart and flow of the various management levels, departments, teams, and other services, you move on to the following steps.

You may be a very high visual person, and the majority of people are. Following is a visual so you can see an overview to give you another perspective of how this works.

All Leaders, Managers & Teams

A step by step system to improve work culture

Step 5
Evaluation of Processes
Pre and Post Training feedback
Assessments
Evaluations, Ongoing support plan

Step 4
Ongoing
Coaching

Step 3
Follow Through
Maintenance

Step 2
Training
Phases

Step 1
Baseline
Observations

Orientation &
Training

STEP 1: Introduction to initiatives,
educating, and preparing for change

Start with the following questions for the organization to get some baseline information. This will provide a starting point, opportunities to educate and tackle any resistance from leadership. You may add, delete, or change more questions into this process depending on the type of company and complexities.

These steps will help you as a guide.

- What are the key drivers or triggers for change? What pain exists within the business? Get a feel for the reality of the costs of incivility within the organization. You can look at things like employee turnover, sick time, and rehiring and training costs to start with.

- How can embedding always behaviors help? Talk to managers about the challenges within their departments around communication barriers and obstacles.

- What are the hot buttons for top management? Identify productivity criteria or other data areas that need immediate attention or intervention.

- Identify key stakeholders and help them to understand what is in it for them, why is this so important what is the overarching goal(s)? This helps to ensure they buy-in for the program, creates understanding, and attaches to outcomes that are important to the business's operational costs and profitability.

- What are the added value or bottom-line benefits for developing behavior standards? Quantify this if possible by looking back at the top two bullets.

- How will everyone know that change is occurring? Establish the success factors that change is happening.

- Identify who has a high level of emotional intelligence and can be advocates of the program? There are many assessments available to identify this competency.

- How will this be communicated or infused within the organization?

Develop a plan, strategy, and timeline for the roll-out and implementation.

STEP 2: Observations and Assessments

Establish a schedule of observations of leadership, managers, and teams to gauge opportunities and hotspots within the organization. Observations will help in establishing a starting point of where people are at and an opportunity to gain valuable information about the culture and provide a perspective for readiness. The person or persons that are chosen to do observations must be neutral parties and understand their role. They also must be excellent communicators and well developed at establishing rapport with a variety of people and personalities. Find and identify the people in your organization who have a high level of emotional intelligence.

The observation phase is one of the most important steps in facilitating change.

It allows the observer to spend time with the people doing the day in day out job responsibilities. You get a chance to see things happen in real-time and how people interact with one another and their customers, clients, or patients. You also get to observe a variety of situations and circumstances of how people handle themselves. This will give you great insight into the emotional health of the company. When you spend time neutrally with people and listen to them, they will develop a comfort level and open up to you. It also gives an opportunity to communicate the goals further, recognize those things that are going well, and find areas that can be improved. These observations can be directly linked back to best practices (i.e., 5 Always Behaviors and Service Recovery) established. When observing people in their day-to-day roles, I have found that they are unaware of their facial expressions, tones, and gestures and have no idea what rapport is and how it is the number one skill to learn to get along.

Following is an example from observations I have made to give you a greater understanding.

In one of my direct observations, I assessed behaviors and communication in a customer service area. I had spent a couple of days there to get to know the people working in this area. It was an extremely busy area with five people working together in the front office. Customer service is the first impression and first point of contact for customers, so it was imperative to set a good tone. If something were to go wrong upon the first contact with a customer or patient, it could derail the rest of the interactions with other departments. Anything going wrong could negatively impact any future business because of how the customer perceived that they were treated. In some cases, it could even determine whether they would continue doing business with that company at all.

The front office staff were all friendly people and very receptive to me being there to observe. I explained why I was there: to observe their strengths according to best practice standards and behaviors. I also made sure they understood that this was a collaborative undertaking and that I needed their feedback because they were an important part of the process. I explained I would also be looking for opportunities to improve internal and external communication.

On my observation materials, I documented everything that I noticed, heard, and felt within various interactions over those few days. Later, I linked them to behavior standards to demonstrate strengths and opportunities, preferring to use the word opportunity instead of weakness because most people associate weakness with something negative. As a coach, my approach is to be a strength and opportunity finder. When working with someone identifying their individual strengths and abilities is always received positively. When discovering opportunities, it is important to do it in a way that the person you're working with uncovers those. This can be easily done with self-assessments linked to best practices. This takes any feeling of being judged out of the process, natural defenses go down, and it allows a person to relax and open up.

Upon completion of the observation phase, this is what I found in the following areas as opportunities to improve the customer experience:

- Incorporate a consistent process of greeting people.

- Develop a process of communicating wait times or giving any detail of what to do upon checking in.

- Provide tone and pitch and body language training to create awareness.

- Create collaboration between colleagues instead

of a rigid perspective of roles to address balancing the workload and increasing team productivity and synergy.

Implementing training in these areas would exponentially increase the department's morale and productivity. The customers they serve would have a great first impression, and customer experience would create rapport, loyalty, and retention.

From this point, I observed and coached other team members and transition points so that everyone was on the same page with behaviors. This ensured that the customers would have a consistent experience and that behaviors were embedded as a company standard. This observation phase was continually followed up to check for obstacles and barriers and keep the team energy engaged and in sync. Together the team would discuss progress and find solutions to barriers together. Everyone was included in the process so that it would be transformative, the change meaningful, and assured it continued consistently. When everyone had a voice within the change, it empowered and placed importance on everyone's views, experiences, talents, and perspectives. This was an all-inclusive process, and the approach offered people the experience of being valued and important.

STEP 3: Train and Develop

In this step, the focus is to educate, reframe, refocus, retrain, and repeat the process.

This step is the time to dive deep into the change process with everyone. Make sure to work with managers and leaders on a schedule and a timeline for implementation. Part of this training process is to fold in experiential training; by this, I mean a hands-on interactive experience. This will give all learning styles a broader view, creating an emotional link to the change. The workshops that are mentioned at the beginning of this chapter would be part of this step's rollout.

In designing and delivering a program, these are important questions to ask everyone throughout the process and help establish that changes are manageable, attainable, and realistic. Again these questions serve as a guideline to help your company with direction.

- Who is best to facilitate training?

- What resources are available now?

- Do the facilitators display the necessary emotional competencies?

- How will I ensure that they do?

- What will be included in the design and how much time will be spent on cognitive versus experiential activities? This is extremely important; people learn more from having an experience; it connects to emotion, which is one of the most powerful influencers.

- How will real-time feedback be incorporated and handled? Make sure to capture feedback in real-time because it is crucial to how the process evolves and matures. How will behavior standards be practiced at work with one another and the people that your company serves?

STEP 4: Follow Up and Maintenance Steps

Follow up is reviewing the process and keeping in mind that the process is ongoing.

This step will provide you with how the program progresses, allow feedback from everyone, reeducate if needed, and adjust if necessary. If there is resistance or obstacles, it is an opportunity to address those. Approach this step in the same manner as the others involving everyone in this assessment and securing agreements around moving forward. Here is a guideline of how to approach this step:

1. Provide on-going coaching and support for a designated period from a neutral party or service. This ensures that the appropriate support is available and accessible during the rollout and training periods.

2. Deliver professional coaching to train trainers within the organization.

3. Develop leadership and management strategies that continually encourage the improvement of behavior standards.

4. Ensure consistency by embedding non-negotiable behaviors as not just an add- on but as the core capabilities for successful performance, productivity, and well- being.

5. Pay attention to areas needing more time as an intervention to address *hotspots* within the

organization.

(

STEP 5: Evaluation of Process

Establish scheduled follow up meeting dates for feedback after a designated period of time. Give enough time so that everyone has had a couple of months of getting used to and comfortable with learning and modeling non-negotiable behaviors. Without feedback, there is no learning and moving forward. Addressing concerns, obstacles, and misunderstandings is information that is a valuable part of the process. This was also addressed in step four but needed to be included in this step to assess for progress. This is the time to decide who will be the designated people who will provide feedback and support from those meetings. This is also a time to decide what form or kind of support there will be to take that information and how it may contribute or alter the processes.

The model below is one that has proven to be highly effective.

The Kirkpatrick Model, developed by Donald Kirkpatrick, is probably the best-known model for analyzing and evaluating the results of training and educational programs.

1. **Immediate reaction:**

   Post-training feedback surveys to gauge people's satisfaction with the program.

2. **Learning:**

   Provide pre- and post-development

assessments (ideally 360 feedback).

3. Behavior:

Conduct appraisals of individual performance and team appraisals of managers.

4. Business performance:

Assess against original critical success factors/benchmarks for behaviors established in the beginning phase.

Suggestion for a wider program evaluation:

- Establish a control group(s) to compare the performance of participants who have been through the training process with that of a similar group who have not.

- Review outcomes and adjust or re-design as needed.

You have in your hands within this chapter a reliable guide to give you a good idea of how, what, where, and why to get a non-negotiable behavior program rolled out. Picking out a name for the program is a good idea. One that I have used is Modeling Behavior Excellence.

No matter who you are, my hope is that what you are reading and learning about in this book is inspiring you to take action. This area of development is so critical to invest in, and well known successful companies have realized the benefits and importance. Linking hard outcomes and results with soft skills produces better results in every facet of the business. Learning how to combine the two to work in partnership will reap massive benefits and success for individuals, teams, and the entire organization.

If you are reading this and in a leadership role, you have an opportunity here to improve or change an entire system. I say create a movement of good behaviors, a culture of excellence to live by, and change lives!

"I suppose leadership at one time meant muscles; but today it means getting along with people."

Mahatma Gandhi

Chapter 11

Stress

Everything that I have written about in this book up to this point has built the case for soft skills and investing in developing programs to increase an organization's emotional competence. I thought it very important to include a chapter about stress because situations and dynamics in a work environment contribute significantly to how people feel about where they work and the level of stress they are under.

Studies and research have shown that a higher level of emotional competence a person has directly impacts a company's profitability and success. The emotional health of any business or company is fostered by the culture represented, which has a direct impact on the well-being of everyone in the workplace.

The paragraph below is by Dr. Gabor Maté, an expert in his field on trauma and chronic stress. In his book

When the Body Says No: Understanding the Stress-Disease Connection, his research covers emotional patterns ingrained in childhood that live in the memory of cells and the brain and appear in interpersonal interactions. Below is a direct quote from Dr. Maté, an excellent description of how stress impacts our interpersonal relationships.

"Emotional competence requires the capacity to feel our emotions, so that we are aware when we are experiencing stress, the ability to express our emotions effectively and thereby to assert our needs and to maintain the integrity of our emotional boundaries. Chronic disruption from stress results in ill health."

Gabor Maté

When the Body Says No: Understanding the Stress-Disease Connection

Stress is a significant component of how it affects our ability to function in life positively. When stress is constant or chronic, it can lead to emotional and physiological issues. I have become increasingly concerned with the impact that stress has on people's emotional and physical health. The focus of a large percentage of clients I see in my private practice is to help alleviate and manage stress. Although some of the stress is generated from home life relationships or other circumstances, a compounding factor comes from their place of work.

I have dedicated a lot of time researching and

learning about the connection between our emotions and our ability to function well depending on the level of stress or the consistency of stress presented in our daily life. Stress is a part of life, and it is important to face that and accept it; however, if stress is chronic, meaning consistent, it can wreak havoc in our life. Learning strategies and techniques to manage stress directly impacts how well we function in life.

Human beings are walking emotions, and learning how to manage those emotions improves our well-being and how we relate and interact with other people. When we feel sad or angry, we release different chemicals into our body than when we feel happy or calm. These chemicals trigger our physical body responses and can either cause harm or create balance and healing. According to the Mayo Clinic and many other case studies, research confirms that our brain releases chemicals into our bodies such as cortisol, adrenaline, and norepinephrine when stress is present. These chemicals can have a negative impact on our bodies when stress is constant or chronic. Imagine that your body is like a bank account. When stress is chronic, it triggers a steady release of cortisol and adrenaline into our bodies, resulting in our natural rhythm being disrupted or out of balance. We then have more negative currency in our bank account, creating a deficit in calming hormones. When you are constantly releasing cortisol and have more of that hormone flowing through your body, it can cause a person to be more on edge and less able to self-regulate emotions. I want to note that cortisol is a very important hormone because it sets off the fight or flight response, which is a survival mechanism intended to keep us safe from danger. The problem is that when it is activated continually by the pressures of daily life, it can cause physical and emotional problems and breakdowns in effective communication with other people. Learning ways to release calming hormones into your body will help counteract an overload of cortisol and improve a person's ability to function better with the demands and pressures of daily life.

Our environment and those places that we spend most of our time, where we live, and work are some of the biggest influences on our health. Since this book is about cultivating a more positive and civil workplace culture and the various impacts of a negative work environment, it is crucial to include insight and create awareness into the significance of how stress affects us.

When people are always stressed out at work, it impacts their ability to do their jobs well and interact with others in a healthy way. Every emotion we have starts as a thought, and that thought automatically produces a feeling in our bodies. Therefore, if the way we think and feel about our environment and relationships is negative and chaotic, stress-producing hormones are being released continuously. This can wreak havoc on our bodies in a variety of areas such as our immune system, nervous system, cardiovascular system, and gastrointestinal system are examples of systems affected by chronic stress. When a person is chronically stressed, or even situationally, some of the physical symptoms experienced are:

- increased heart rate

- elevated blood pressure

- headaches

- muscle tension and more

- low energy

- aches and pains

Along with the physiological impacts, there are emotional ones as well.

Some of the effects of how chronic stress affects our emotional state are:

- sleeplessness

- nervousness

- irritability

- inability to concentrate

- anger

- restlessness

- poor memory

Laurel Mellin, an American author of nine books focusing on brain-based health, stress overload, and stress eating, wrote *The Pathway,* included on the *New York Times Best Sellers* list. Mellin is also the founder of Emotional Brain Training in Larkspur, California, a program designed to rewire stress and promote resilience. In her research, she demonstrates how stress affects our brain function, and the more stressed we are, our ability to function and interact with other people declines. Mellin's research substantiates that when we feel good and things are going well, we are operating in a higher region of the brain. As stress is introduced, a person's ability to function declines, and as it does, so do all other aspects of how we relate in life. More information on Mellin's work on Emotional Brain Training and be found at ebt.org, which is an extensive support program to help teach and train people to manage chronic stress.

One way that employee satisfaction is measured at work is how well the people get along with each other and the quality of those relationships. One of the reasons that recognizing the effects of chronic stress becomes even more important is that stress is a factor in most jobs. Depending on the position, it may be a very consistent amount of stress or situational. If the quality of the relationships between coworkers is good, it helps alleviate the stress of the workload and demands instead of adding to it. People that are stressed tend to exhibit shortness and sometimes rude behavior. They also have more difficulty concentrating on their tasks, which translates to a higher chance of error. Depending on the profession, this can add up to more than wasted dollars and efforts; it can cause harm. Incorporating good behavior standards helps people improve their peer and coworker relationships, which helps alleviate or lessen the feelings of stress and overload from the demands of the job.

Let's use the medical field as an example of a workplace where an error could be caused by stress. If a clinician under chronic stress is distracted or disengaged, they may accidentally give an incorrect dosage of medicine or too quickly advise a patient on how to take their medication. Another example might be forgetting to note an important change in a patient's condition or being distracted and not noticing an important change in that patient's condition. These are just a few examples of many scenarios that could cause harm in a medical situation. Or what about the executive that has to make important decisions about a company's financial future and weigh in with a myriad of details to make these decisions. This takes experience and the skill of understanding how to make decisions affecting the success of the company and takes a lot of emotional competence. Understanding things like how those decisions impact the employees and customers, what are the important influences to weigh in on, and how these decisions get communicated are imperative to how positively or negatively the information is received by your team. Leaders who know how to relate well to their advisors and create an atmosphere of camaraderie and open communication are likely to make decisions that are well thought through because they have established good relationships. Suppose people work in a culture of fear where decisions are made without consideration or open communication with parties involved. In that case, the lack of communication can create barriers that result in confusion or misinformation. This situation can result in a considerable amount of stress for everyone involved as people create their own stories, including their individual concerns and fears. Understandably, sharing information has to be balanced appropriately depending on the impact the decisions may have on the people working within the company. I wrote about the difference between transactional leadership and transformational leadership in chapter ten. A fusion of both logic and emotional competence can provide a better outcome, even if the message is a difficult one. I have worked in a few environments and observed environments where people were afraid to express themselves for fear of losing their job or being criticized or labeled as difficult or disruptive. This puts people in a difficult position to work. The option is to find another job, which is more stressful, or try to deal with uncertainty, causing more stress within the company.

Frequently, companies experience much greater absenteeism as people call in sick to avoid stress at work. Along with absenteeism, work productivity declines and engagement, and turnover increases.

Since more and more people are retiring later in life as life expectancy has increased, so does the rising costs of medical insurance and social security.

Companies that promote a positive work culture are becoming more and more attractive to people as they have to work much longer than years ago to retire and collect benefits.

Stress is a part of life, so learning how to manage stress effectively is an excellent strategy for any person's well-being. Since stress is unavoidable as many situations or circumstances in life are out of our control, having the ability and skills to improve your emotional state will improve every part of your life. When stress reduction is promoted and implemented in a work environment, the benefits to the company are significant to the bottom line. Investing in stress programs can save thousands and thousands of dollars.

Bill walked into work Monday morning with a pit in his stomach. He had been feeling this way for months now. The department manager was extremely busy, and people felt the pressure as the company had a series of layoffs in the past year. For months the workload had been over the top, and a few people had quit because they were tired of the long hours and were in constant fear of being let go. There was a lot of confusion within the company around the layoffs and rumors that the company was in financial jeopardy. The layoffs had decreased the staff but increased the amount of work required to maintain productivity. The employees in Bill's department were spending a lot of time talking and worrying about the next lay off and concerned about the uncertainty and how it was taking a toll on morale. Many people called in sick regularly, which increased the burden even more on the people who had to cover even more of the workload. Bill had always prided himself on being a loyal employee and always tried to look for the silver lining in any situation. Being a manager was a position that he envisioned for many years, and he had worked hard for the promotion. He loved what he did for work but had not really thought much about the conditions of the environment prior to the past year. Bill had always been focused on learning and becoming competent at what it took to perform his jobs' particular skill set. Since graduating from college, he had worked at this company and witnessed many changes but never as a manager. Bill did not know what to do to help his staff, and he could not seem to get clear direction from the top leadership that he could convey to help put people at ease. The pressure was on Bill to keep the productivity levels up. He was also challenged with improving employee morale and engagement even though the company was reducing staff and cutting budgets. Since the layoffs had been going on for almost a year, people were starting to show the effects of the additional demands and the uncertainty, so stress was very high. Almost everyone had become edgy at the office, and people were really short with one another, and attention to detail was slipping. People were also very sensitive to any feedback around errors. Every night Bill went home and felt worn out and exhausted from the emotional environment at work. He was not sleeping well, and his wife pointed out that he had been more quiet and distracted. She felt that Bill seemed and acted unhappily and even noticed him being impatient with the children.

This stressed Bill out even more because he knew that the quality of his home life was being impacted, and he felt horrible. Bill thought a lot about what to do; he felt helpless and alone. He never imagined having his dream job and feeling so miserable. Unless something changed soon, Bill felt he would be forced to search for other employment.

This story is one that probably resonates with many people reading this now. It is not enough that we are good at our jobs and have the skills and experience to do it well;

if our environment is unhealthy, it can challenge every aspect of our lives. Our emotions are powerful, and when not attended to, will override logic every time. Natural stress responses go back years to man's early existence; it was a primal response to a potential threat or danger, a very important response that was part of keeping us safe when wild animals were lurking everywhere. As humans have evolved through time, we do not have to hunt or gather for our food and be on the watch for constant threat or danger to our existence. The feeling of threat triggers the same response and fires the same chemicals in our bodies. The stresses in today's life are much more complex and much more prevalent, although not imminent danger for the most part. This is why having a strategy to deal with the daily pressure, demands, and responsibilities are so important.

If you are a business owner or in a leadership role, I invite you to think about how the work environment could benefit from addressing stress proactively. If you are not in a managerial or supervisory role, I also invite you to think about a strategy for yourself to help you alleviate and manage stress in your life so you can feel like you're more in control of regulating your emotions in any situation.

Whichever role you are in, recommend, or introduce a monthly or biweekly workshop on stress management for everyone to gather ideas and information to help them. Investing in stress reduction for your employees will model that you acknowledge related stress and, more importantly, care about each others' well-being and be willing to provide support.

Chapter 12

Moving Forward

In this book, you have read all aspects of the hard case for soft skills in the work environment. Creating a more civil work environment is one of the biggest opportunities to improve a company's success and profitability; after all, most people spend a great deal of time at work. In my opinion, the bigger picture is contributing to the well-being of the people in this world. Making civility a priority has a major ripple effect as people often have a tendency to bring work home with them. Many of the chapters provided insight into how behavior affects us and simple things you can do to improve any relationship by living by certain behaviors. In the world we live in today, incivility is rampant in our society. How we interact and socialize with one another has changed so much and has become, in many ways, less personal. It is not uncommon to not know your neighbor or get together with your community regularly. How we communicate primarily is through social media, texting, emailing, or via remote conferencing. Technology and the age of information have allowed many ways to be in touch with one another anywhere and at any time; however, it is also contributed to a loss of feeling of connection to one another. This high tech world makes it easier to take for granted face to face communication with other people.

The fast pace of today's world has us rushing and running from one thing to another, and we are often in the company of strangers. In some ways, this makes it easier not to get personal or be short or rude to people we do not know. Our culture has become more diverse, and so the possibility of cross-cultural misunderstandings and conflict is always present. Situations like school bullying, anger over parking spaces, cell phones pinging us anytime and anywhere, internet trolling, yelling supervisors, upset air travelers, road rage, snappy and stressed out people are commonplace in our world. So what do we do? What is the answer?

The answer is simple, embrace civility, take a moment, stop, think about your actions or reactions, and take responsibility for your behavior. Interacting with other human beings is one of the most important things that we do in life. The very essence of who we are at a fundamental level is about connection. One would think that improving the quality of our interactions should be a top priority? It would certainly make for a better quality of life, a happier, healthier, and more meaningful one.

Lowering stress in the workplace is an excellent way

to contribute to humanity. How we set our standards as human beings, how we treat one another everyday impacts every facet of our lives and with the people with whom we interact. Every single human encounter has a consequence. Think about people who have crossed your path and have touched you somehow, perhaps people you knew for a long time or a very brief time. Some of the people that have made the biggest impression on me were very brief. Every day is an opportunity to smile at someone, listen to them, acknowledge them. Why not share in a way that intentionally is the best in you?

I grew up in a small rural town in northern Maine, where everyone seemed to know each other. I consider myself to have been a latch key kid. Most everyone in my town kept their doors unlocked when I was growing up, and it was not uncommon for people to leave their keys in their cars. Where I grew up, there were no big cities for hours, and it was two lanes and lots of dirt roads to get there from our town. I used to ride my bike as a kid from one town to another using the backroads. It was really that safe. Not that we had an occasional event requiring law intervention, but everything was predictable and safe for the most part. This will provide you with some context for the next part of this story.

Quite a few years ago, I was traveling in a city unfamiliar to me. I decided to take an evening walk and asked the concierge how to get to a popular park not far away. He gave me directions referencing city blocks: go two blocks, take a right and go another block and then take another right and go left and it will be right in front of you. Although I was confused by his directions because growing up, we did not give directions in blocks, I thought to myself about how confusing this was to me but did not want to tell him I did not know what a block was. Soon after I strolled out, I became disoriented and confused about where I was and started second-guessing my route. The more I walked, the more the very busy streets became deserted and narrow. Suddenly, I heard police sirens and saw flashing lights; up ahead, I saw a police officer jump out of his car and come running down the alley, I was walking along. My immediate thought was one of relief. I soon realized he was going into the building just ahead of me and was not noticing me.

Scared, I ran until I came out on another street that was busy with people. But no one was making eye contact, I felt invisible. Finally, a woman who I approached gave me directions. She looked me in the eyes and calmly and kindly explained that it was really easy. I was very close to where I wanted to go and reviewed the directions. I was beyond grateful. I don't think this woman had any idea what her act of kindness meant to me that evening. Although this was many years ago, to this day, I will always remember her and can see her face in my mind.

This story's moral is you never honestly know how much a moment of kindness can impact a person's life. Every action causes an effect. It is like throwing a pebble into a lake; the energy of that ripple continues to move and affect the entire body of water.

Be kind, be well, *behavior self.*

For more information regarding programs contact:

amber@workculturesolutions.com

or go to:

www.workculturesolutions.com

Bibliography

Goleman, D. (2020). *Emotional intelligence.* London:

Bloomsbury.

HBR guide to emotional intelligence. (2017). Boston, MA: Harvard Business Review Press.

Instaread. (2015). *The Body Keeps the Score: Brain, Mind, and Body in the Healing of Trauma by Bessel van der Kolk, MD | Key Takeaways, Analysis & Review.* San Francisco: IDreamBooks.

Lipton, B. H. (2016). *The biology of belief: Unleashing the power of consciousness, matter & miracles.* Carlsbad, CA: Hay House.

Maté, G. (2019). *When the body says no: The cost of hidden stress.* Brunswick, Victoria, Australia: Scribe.

Mellin, L. (2004). *The pathway: Follow the road to health and happiness*. New York: ReganBooks.

Schwartz, J., & Gladding, R. (2012). *You are not your brain: The 4-step solution for changing bad habits, ending unhealthy thinking, and taking control of your life*. New York: Penguin Group.

Studer, Q., Robinson, B. C., & Cook, K. (2010). *The HC-AHPS handbook: Hardwire your hospital for pay-for-performance success*. Gulf Breeze, FL: Fire Starter Pub.

Website Resources:

https://www.nlp-techniques.org/what-is-nlp/senses-submodalities/

https://www.simplypsychology.org/multiple-intelli-gences.html

https://www.simplypsychology.org/big-five-personali-ty.html

https://smallbusiness.chron.com/transformational-lead-ership-vs-transactional-leadership-definition

https://www.cnbc.com/2017/10/12/a-majority-of-men-say-there-are-enough-women-in-leadership-roles.html https://www.huffpost.com/entry/the-top-10-emotional-lyint_b_911576